Highpointing for Tibet

Highpointing for
Tibet

*A Journey Supporting
The Rowell Fund*

———————————
—————

Dr. Steve Gardiner with John Jancik

———

Forewords by Richard Gere and Conrad Anker

Copyright 2017 by Quiet Water Publishing, LLC
www.quietwaterpublishing.com

ISBN-13: 978-1-947427-07-5
ISBN-10: 1-947427-07-5

All rights reserved. No part of this book may be reproduced in any form without written permission from the publisher.

Note: The names of people and places in this book are factual. The events have been presented as accurately as possible based on field notes, journals, and other records.

Disclaimer: Highpointing can be a dangerous activity. Many of the climbs in this book require the use of mountain climbing skills and techniques. Participating in these activities can lead to injury or death. Anyone attempting to climb mountains is responsible for obtaining the proper training, gaining adequate physical fitness, and learning how to use the necessary equipment proficiently. Weather, seasonal changes, forces of nature, land ownership, and other concerns may affect the condition of a climbing route or safe access to a highpoint. Neither the publisher or the authors assume any responsibility for incidents that may occur to individuals who attempt to complete any of the travels or climbs described in this book.

Front Cover
In the spirit of 50 for Tibet, John Jancik, left, and Steve Gardiner celebrate reaching the summit of the Rock of Gibraltar overlooking the Mediterranean Sea. Photo by Jessica Morse.

(Inset photo). Galen and Barbara Rowell meet with His Holiness the 14th Dalai Lama in Dharamsala, India. Photo courtesy of Mountain Light Photography, Inc.

Back Cover
(Left) After finishing the climb up the snowy summit pyramid of Kebnekaise in Sweden, John Jancik, left, and Steve Gardiner look back at the route they just successfully climbed. Photo by Jessica Morse.

(Center) Team members approach the large crevasse on Mount Rainier in Washington. They were eventually able to pass over the crevasse on a narrow, exposed snow bridge. Photo by John Jancik.

(Right) After eight attempts over a thirty-year span, John Jancik (right) shares a moment of joy on the summit of Granite Peak in Montana with Steve Gardiner. Photo courtesy of John Jancik.

*To the spirit of the Tibetan people who are
struggling to maintain their language,
culture, religion, and identity.
May they find their freedom
through compassion and peace.*

The Rowell Fund for Tibet has been very successful in its mission to encourage and support the work of many talented Tibetans in communicating issues of importance to their community to a broader Tibetan and international audience.

Through the medium of photography, film-making, writing, journalism, and many other projects supported by **The Rowell Fund for Tibet**, Tibetans have been empowered to express themselves.

This wonderful book tells the story of how a small group of motivated individuals, touched by the beauty of Tibetan culture, can make a big difference to the lives of many.

The International Campaign for Tibet supports the preservation of the unique Tibetan culture and identity through a multi-throng approach, which includes original research, communication, advocacy, and empowerment of Tibetan communities. We are proud and honored to continue to support **The Rowell Fund for Tibet** and strongly recommend this beautiful book.

Matteo Mecacci, President
The International Campaign for Tibet

Contents

FOREWORD by Richard Gere... xi

FOREWORD by Conrad Anker... xii

ACKNOWLEDGEMENTS by Steve Gardiner.................... xiv

ACKNOWLEDGEMENTS by John Jancik......................... xv

PROLOGUE by John Jancik.. 1

CHAPTER 1. Climbing for a Cause...................................... 9

CHAPTER 2. The Top of the American Southwest............. 19

CHAPTER 3. The Top of New England................................29

CHAPTER 4. The Top of the Northwest.............................. 41

CHAPTER 5. The Dalai Lama.. 53

CHAPTER 6. The First Year of 50 for Tibet........................ 63

CHAPTER 7. The Top of Montana....................................... 73

CHAPTER 8. Nearest the Sun... 83

CHAPTER 9. The Top of the British Isles............................. 93

CHAPTER 10. The Top of Scandinavia................................ 99

CHAPTER 11. The Top of Japan.. 115

CHAPTER 12. The Top of Iberia... 125

CHAPTER 13. Yosemite National Park................................ 137

CHAPTER 14. ECHO Geophysical Corporation................... 145

CHAPTER 15. A Matter of Seconds..................................... 153

CHAPTER 16. The Top of the Maritime Provinces............. 165

EPILOGUE by John Jancik... 175

ABOUT THE AUTHORS.. 182

APPENDIX A.	Donations..184
APPENDIX B.	Contact Information............................ 185
APPENDIX C.	Suggested Reading............................... 186
APPENDIX D.	Letter of Support-Gov. Ritter............. 187
APPENDIX E.	Letter of Support-Mark Udall............ 188
APPENDIX F.	Letter of Support-ICT......................... 189
APPENDIX G.	Letter of Support-Jimmy Chin........... 190

"Wherever I live, I shall feel homesick for Tibet. I often think I can still hear the cries of wild geese and cranes and the beating of their wings as they fly over Lhasa in the clear, cold moonlight. My heartfelt wish is that my story may create some understanding for a people whose will to live in peace and freedom has won so little sympathy from an indifferent world."
--- Heinrich Harrer, *Seven Years in Tibet*

"Contrary to popular belief, no mountaineer discovers the meaning of life—or even lesser insights—at the top of a peak. As with other events in a person's life, reflection comes later when the excitement is gone. Only then do summit moments take on meanings beyond the obvious."
--- Galen Rowell, *Mountains of the Middle Kingdom*

Foreword
by Richard Gere

Mountains have defined the Tibetan people historically with Tibetans referring to Tibet as a place surrounded by a fence of Snow Mountains.

It is also mountains and their love of mountains that have also led many people throughout the world to first learn about Tibet, understand its culture, religion and people, and subsequently become strong supporters. The book, *Highpointing For Tibet: A Journey Supporting The Rowell Fund*, is the story of one such group of people, led by John Jancik.

Tibet's precious culture and religion, with its principles of wisdom and compassion and its message of interdependence and nonviolence, are rooted in the Tibetan landscape and Tibetan hearts. This culture has much to contribute to the development of the world civilization. Therefore, the survival of Tibetan Buddhist knowledge is vital for the world, as well as the Tibetan people.

Change will come to Tibet; it is not a matter of if, but when. It may take time, but we need to act. As His Holiness the Dalai Lama has said change can only take place through action. We each have a role to play, and the friends of the Tibetan people, who have shared their experience in this book, are playing their roles.

Foreword
by Conrad Anker

Climbing is hard work. What starts as a dream requires planning, teamwork, proper equipment, long days, and good weather. Your team has to wake up early, endure cold, deal with petty annoyances, and learn how to evaluate risk. Every step is against gravity. It's something that you want. It isn't easy.

If you're determined, you'll find a pace to suit your team, experience nature, catch a sublime sunrise, and if you are lucky, make it to the summit. It will be a well-earned moment with your friends. The experiences that make life special. The ones that you remember for the rest of your life. Yet mountaineering isn't for everyone. There is a degree of hardship and risk that brings out, for those that have found a calling, a sense of purpose and dedication. It's what we live for.

Highpointing is about recognizing a geographic spot, one that through the forces of nature has risen above the surrounding plains and hills. While the points are known, you can look at them on your handheld computer, if you want to experience them - from the squeaky cold snow and thin air of Denali to the humid forested hummock of Louisiana – you have to dedicate your life to climbing, making them a priority. The unknown of climbing these peaks lies in the journey. The people one meets, the challenges one addresses, and the unexpected vistas are the essence of a journey. In this day and age, you won't discover new lands, you'll discover yourself and break any preconceived boundaries.

John Jancik, a friend of the late adventure photographer Galen Rowell, connects this journey of discovery with the people of Tibet. Galen and his wife Barbara were connected to Tibet in a meaningful manner. After their passing in 2002, the Rowell family and friends established The Rowell Fund for Tibet, an annual grant cycle to encourage and support Tibetan artists. In many ways, the journey of the Tibetan artist is similar to mountaineering. The hardship isn't self-imposed and the challenges in many instances are external, yet the reward of trying something unknown has its intrinsic rewards. By combining a personal quest for the 50 highpoints in the United States and the artists of Tibet, John has added purpose to this journey of self-discovery.

Immerse yourself into John's story. It's a fine way to see the highpoints from a fresh perspective and think about how, regardless of who you are or where you are from, we are all connected.

Be good, be kind, be happy.

Conrad Anker

Bozeman, Montana

Acknowledgements
by Steve Gardiner

John Jancik created the idea to reach all fifty state highpoints. His wife, Terri Baker, supported the plan, and the two of them, along with their company, ECHO Geophysical Corporation, funded the project. Otherwise, none of these adventures, nor this book, would have happened.

Thanks to the International Campaign for Tibet for creating The Rowell Fund for Tibet to honor Galen and Barbara Rowell, and for their support of our 50 for Tibet project. ICT's framework provided the foundation we needed to launch and live our project.

For providing unwavering support to The Rowell Fund and for writing excellent forewords for this book, we send thanks to actor Richard Gere and climber Conrad Anker.

Our appreciation goes out to Jim Thomsen of Jim Thomsen Creative for his sharp editorial eye and comments that helped make this a much better book. Brian Zimmerman of Cre843 did a masterful job of capturing our ideas in his cover design.

Thanks also to the many people who went with us on the highpointing trips, signed the Rowell book, held the flags, took photos, shared our concern for the people of Tibet, and in many other ways made the efforts of 50 for Tibet a joy and a success.

I am happy that my wife, Peggy, and my daughters, Greta, Romney, and Denby, were all able to join us for parts of the 50 for Tibet project. My thanks and love to each of them for supporting my participation in the journeys and my work on this book.

Acknowledgements
by John Jancik

First and foremost, I would like to thank my wife Terri who has been solidly behind the 50 For Tibet fundraising adventure since it started. Simply put, without her support and participation, this journey of ten-plus years would have never been realized. I will forever be grateful. I would also like to thank my other Team HighPoint teammates Steve Gardiner and David Baker. Their enthusiasm and determination to carry on 50 For Tibet has been quite remarkable. With so many miles we have logged around the world together, it is hard to imagine highpointing without you.

The list of other individuals who I would like to acknowledge is quite lengthy but I would be remiss not to note John Ackerly, Tencho Gyatso, Joe Sears, Bill Finch, Juli Parrott, Lizzy Ludwig, Alli Bannias, John Mitchler, Nicole Rowell Ryan and Tony Rowell. Their enthusiastic support and participation in various different ways in the 50 For Tibet fundraising adventure has been more than ever hoped for. Thank you!

In addition, the staff of the International Campaign For Tibet and the Advisory Board for The Rowell Fund for Tibet have both been most gracious and supportive of this book project. I would also like to thank Steve Siguaw for helping out on several facets of this book and getting it off the ground. Your book about sailing around the world, *Voyage Into Hell*, ignited my enthusiasm to have the 50 For Tibet story told in some fashion. To those of you that I have not named but know that you have been a part of 50 For Tibet and The Rowell Fund For Tibet, your participation will always be remembered.

Lastly, U2's songs were a constant companion for me from Hawaii to Ireland to Australia to the Canary Islands. From *Where The Streets Have No Name* to *Beautiful Day*, the songs brought energy to me.

Galen Rowell climbs a rocky slope with a friend. The Rowell Fund is named in memory of Galen and his wife Barbara.
Photo by Tony Rowell.

Prologue
by John Jancik

This book is a story about two ideas, The Rowell Fund For Tibet and 50 For Tibet. Their paths intertwined for a cause named in honor and memory of two incredibly gifted individuals. While The Rowell Fund and 50 For Tibet goals became common ground in 2006, their origins are from different times and from different reasons. It is from there I begin this story.

Galen Rowell, Robert F. Kennedy and John Denver are heroes of mine. They all share two things that I greatly admire in people—passion and determination. With those two traits, humans can achieve success beyond all expectations. While I never met Robert F. Kennedy or John Denver, I was gifted to not only meet Galen but explore the northernmost land on Earth with him.

Galen Rowell was born on August 23, 1940, in Oakland, California. At age thirty-two, he became a full-time photographer. He eventually pioneered a new kind of photography in which he was not merely an observer, but considered himself a participant in the scenes that he photographed. He considered the landscape part of the adventure, and the adventure part of the landscape. Combined with his love of climbing, whether it would be first ascents in the Sierra Nevada Mountains or speed records up Denali (Mount McKinley) and Mount Kilimanjaro, Galen had the opportunity to see and be part of the environment he captured on film. Few, if any, could match the achievements of what Galen was accomplishing on film or in the mountaineering world in those years.

In 1977, Galen's book *In the Throne Room of the Mountain*

Gods, about the history of mountaineering on K2, was published and is considered a classic of mountaineering literature. His 1986 book *Mountain Light: In Search of the Dynamic Landscape* is one of the best-selling how-to photo books of all time. By the early 1990s, Galen had firmly established himself as one of the premier photographers and climbers of his generation.

Late in 1995, as co-leader of the 1996 American Top Of The World Expedition ten-member team that was going to northern Greenland, I was searching for potential team members to fill out the roster. One teammate from Berkeley mentioned that he knew Galen and asked if it would be okay to invite him to join us. I was ecstatic. I knew about Galen's amazing accomplishments, and his incredible books lined my shelves. I needed no introduction to him; no climbing resume, no references. Galen was in his own universe. My expedition co-leader, Ken Zerbst said: "For me it gave us (the expedition) credibility. The fact that someone with Galen's credentials would be interested in participating in our expedition and doing a piece for *LIFE* magazine meant we were embarking on a very exciting and unique geographic adventure that indeed would capture people's attention."

The 1996 American Top Of The World Expedition lived up to its name as it discovered a new northerly piece of terra firma which Galen did indeed document for *LIFE* magazine. We also accomplished first ascents of the two highest peaks in the previously unexplored H.H. Benedict Range that lies along the northern Greenland coast, some four hundred-plus miles from the North Pole. By all hopes of the team members, the expedition returned home a major success story.

However, being on the expedition and getting to know Galen on a more personal level than reading his books was a special treat for me. At one time, early in the expedition, Galen and I were photographing an Arctic fox that was curious about us (perhaps the first people it had ever seen?). The fox walked over to Galen's tripod-mounted camera and marked it with his urine. Instead of being upset, Galen turned to me, smiled and said, "Well, at least he couldn't reach the camera!"

A Journey Supporting The Rowell Fund

As a geologist by academic training, I spent hours on the expedition talking with Galen about the world of geology, whether it was North Peary Land, Greenland, or his beloved Sierra Nevada Mountains in California. Galen's insatiable appetite for knowledge and his natural curiosity made conversations entertaining and intriguing. In his younger days, Galen had collected minerals and rocks. Our interests in the complex sphere of geology had crossed paths.

Over the years after the expedition, Galen and I stayed in touch; however, our paths only occasionally crossed (usually while my wife Terri Baker and I were visiting the Bay Area). In late 2000, Terri and I, as co-leaders of a new expedition, talked with him about returning to northern Greenland during July 2001. Unfortunately, Galen had already made a previous commitment during that time. However, he did provide a critical reference for a mountaineer, Vernon Tejas, who is a legend for his Seven Summit (climbing the highest peak on each continent) achievements. Vernon would go on to become a major positive contributor to the 2001 Return To The Top Of The World Expedition, which made several first ascents and the second climb ever of the highest peak (Helvetia Tinde) in the northernmost mountain range on Earth.

However, Galen's influence on the 2001 expedition did not stop with his being just a reference. In 1996, during an expedition rest day along the northern coast of Greenland, I walked up to Galen, who was attentively studying air photographs of the region. He was attempting to figure out which mountain along the north coast was the northernmost mountain on Earth. After determining that there were a multitude of candidates near Sands Fjord, the conclusion was that some expedition would have to climb them all and GPS-document their latitudes to determine which was the actual northernmost. In 2001, the expedition became the first to do exactly that.

After returning home from northern Greenland in the summer of 2001, Steve Gardiner (a fellow 1996 and 2001 northern Greenland expeditions teammate) from Billings, Montana, and I wrote a book titled *Under The Midnight Sun*. This project, which covered our two adventures to the northernmost land and mountain ranges on

Earth, was the exclamation point on two expeditions that pioneered climbing and exploration in a land relatively unexplored by man. For me, it was a challenging project, as I had never attempted to write a book before. However, knowing that the stories from the two expeditions had met with true appreciation and enjoyment when I gave slide shows about the adventures, I believed that readers would potentially be delighted with a book about the daring and exciting accomplishments of the expedition teams.

Not long after Steve and I began the book project, it was obvious to us as well as the book's publisher that Galen's photographic work from the 1996 expedition would be a tremendous addition to it. Galen, who readily agreed to contribute to the book when I talked to him about the possibility, began submitting photographs almost immediately. My excitement to have his photographs published with Steve's and my writing was a dream come true for me. However, tragically and shockingly, while the book was being prepared for printing at the publishing house, Galen and his wife Barbara lost their lives in a plane crash near their home in Bishop, California, on August 11, 2002. Shocked and deeply saddened, Terri quickly wrote a passage, "In Memoriam," on behalf of her 1996 and 2001 northern Greenland expedition teammates for Galen and Barbara to be included in *Under The Midnight Sun*. This last-second addition to the book, while wonderfully written, left me without joy. Galen would never see the book I had co-written and which featured his wonderful work on the front cover. Like many people, I was heartbroken.

Galen and Barbara's deaths were a major loss to the photographic and climbing communities. Each were accomplished authors and outstanding in their respective fields of endeavor. However, they were much more than that. Caring people, whether it would be about the environment or the issues surrounding Tibetans, Galen and Barbara were passionate participants in their beliefs. In Galen's own written words: "My life's goal is not to publish as much as possible, but to make a difference." Out of their passion, Galen compiled a wonderful book titled *My Tibet* in which His Holiness the 14th Dalai Lama wrote quotations for one hundred and eight photographs that

Galen had taken during his multiple visits to Tibet. This piece of work introduced Tibet to thousands of people around the world. The book remains one, if not the best, of Galen and Barbara's many published books.

From the grief of Galen and Barbara's family members, friends and the International Campaign for Tibet (ICT) staff arose an idea to create a fund in the Rowells' name (The Rowell Fund For Tibet). John Ackerly, then ICT president, and a close friend of Galen and Barbara, conceived the concept and presented it to friends Bob Palais, Justin Black and Conrad Anker, as well as Galen's daughter, Nicole Rowell Ryan. The purpose of this fund would be to support Tibetans worldwide who can make a valuable contribution to their community and/or an international audience in the fields of visual arts and media, and environmental and women's rights. John Ackerly commented, "Lodi Gyari (Special Envoy of His Holiness the Dalai Lama, based in Washington D.C.) was very supportive of the idea, which was key, as it took my time away from other ICT work. He always felt that Tibet's environmental issues didn't get enough attention and admired Galen for publicly speaking out, when few others would."

In 2004, the fund's first grants were awarded. Mountaineer and author David Breashears, who is also on the newly formed Advisory Board for The Rowell Fund for Tibet, said, "These awards highlight the broad range and diversity of work being undertaken by Tibetans to promote and develop their cultural heritage. This vital work is a worthy tribute to Galen and Barbara's passion and commitment to the Tibetan cause."

John Ackerly reflected on that time: "From the start, the fundraising was a bit harder than I expected, but we kept getting such good feedback from the Tibetan community. We also wanted to show that we were willing to fund unusual and even risky projects—not just things with the stamp of approval of the Tibetan government in exile."

In 2005, in what would become another life-changing event for me, Terri and I became members of the advisory board for The Rowell Fund for Tibet. The support to participate came from the head of the Board, John Ackerly, and my fellow 1996 American-Top Of The World expedition teammate (and board member) Bob Palais. Other board members included Conrad Anker, Jimmy Chin, Tony Rowell, Nicole Rowell Ryan, Beth Cushman and Justin Black. It was quite an honor to join such an accomplished and talented group of individuals to work on the fund. This incredible opportunity to make a difference for people halfway around the world would soon overlap with my interest in another activity that was new to me—highpointing.

In late summer of 2005, I began pondering a quest to reach all fifty state highpoints in less than a year. While the record for doing so was in less time than that, my goal was intertwined with still running my thirty-person company, ECHO Geophysical Corporation. This would not be easy, with all the hours I was used to putting in at work. But actually achieving the goal would be less important than the fun I'd have in trying.

As the 2005 summer turned to autumn, my dream of a highpointing adventure began to expand. Terri would join me as her schedule as a hospice physician would allow. Terri's son David Baker, a teammate on the 2001 Return To The Top Of The World Expedition, joined. Steve Gardiner was in, too, as his Billings Senior High School teaching schedule would provide. Team HighPoint was born.

I proposed the idea that we turn the highpointing adventure into a fundraiser for The Rowell Fund for Tibet. It was an interesting idea that Team HighPoint philosophically agreed had potential to raise significant monies for The Rowell Fund as well as give the highpointing an "outside" purpose with its existence. The marriage of highpointing with The Rowell Fund seemed like a perfect match. As this idea took shape, David came up with the motto the newly born 50 For Tibet highpoint team would use in its travels: "Celebrating One Mountain Culture To Preserve Another." It was the perfect way to describe our feelings about our upcoming adventures.

Before Team HighPoint started though, we wanted approval for the concept from the The Rowell Fund's advisory board. So, in November 2005, Terri and I traveled to Washington, D.C. to visit with a majority of the Board at the International Campaign for

Tibet's offices. Enthusiastic, board members also proposed doing a financial-contributor participation climb of Mount Whitney (14,505 feet) in June 2006, in conjunction with Team HighPoint's ascent of the first state in our quest. It was a natural fit. The coincidence that Mount Whitney, in California, Galen and Barbara's home state, had been climbed by Galen numerous times, was not lost on anyone.

Soon after returning from Washington, D.C., we organized plans for 50 For Tibet's launch in June 2006. A website was built (with a Facebook page coming later) and intense training began. In addition, figuring out the logistics to reach 50 state highpoints in a limited period of time—with most planned for the summer and autumn of 2006—was no small task. I needed to plan my absence from my business. And we worked on ways of reaching out to potential contributors to The Rowell Fund.

As the spring of 2006 rolled by, the organization, training and logistics fell into place. Two experts—Diane Winger, co-author of *Highpointing Adventures*; and John Mitchler of the Highpointers Club—served as my encyclopedia for questions regarding highpointing around the U.S. While I had already done highpoints like Mount Whitney (where I first met Terri in 1990) and Timms Hill in Wisconsin (my home state), I knew very little about highpointing in many other states. Some state highpoints are privately held, some highpoint mountains only have access with permits, and some highpoints can be readily reached only during certain months.

Besides the facts and information provided by Diane and John, they were also an inspiration to me for their enthusiasm for the highpointing concept. Highpointing was still a growing idea in the U.S., with fewer individuals completing all fifty states than successfully summiting Mount Everest. John Mitchler, who completed all fifty states in 2003, explained, "Although a few folks like the challenge of doing the fifty highpoints quickly, it takes twenty years for most people to do the necessary traveling, so we see people come and go over the years, as their interest level varies and schedules allow."

While Team HighPoint was not going to be exploring new lands—unlike our 1996 and 2001 northern Greenland expeditions—

we were going to be setting out on a year-long adventure that would consume vast amounts of time, energy and money. In fact, all monies raised during the 50 For Tibet fundraiser adventure would go directly to ICT and The Rowell Fund for Tibet with all the expenses for the highpointing adventure being paid for by ECHO Geophysical as well as Terri and me.

As May turned into June 2006, excitement for the start of the 50 For Tibet fundraising adventure grew. A Denver television station, CBS affiliate KCNC-TV, interviewed Team HighPoint and ran a feature piece on 50 For Tibet. John Ackerly and world-renowned mountaineer Conrad Anker committed to the Mount Whitney fundraising climb. In addition, one of Galen's longtime climbing partners, Peter Croft, elected to join the group. Galen's son, Tony Rowell, joined as well. John, Conrad, Peter, and Tony—as well as others—would climb Mount Whitney via The Mountaineer's Route while Team HighPoint & Friends (including David's sister Jessica) elected for the 22-mile-long, one-day climb via the Mount Whitney Trail. If all went as planned, the two groups would meet each other on the summit midday on June 16.

On June 14, David, Steve, Jessica, and I met at the Denver International Airport for our flight to Reno, Nevada, to officially begin 50 For Tibet. It was a nervous time for me as I knew that many weeks and months had gone into the preparation for the upcoming fundraising adventure. I was anxious about our climbing schedule, as the first leg of highpointing around the U.S. would be a climb every other day for the first four states of California, Nevada, Arizona and New Mexico. More than 34,000 feet of elevation would be gained and descended over seven days. Rest days would mean driving from one state to another. Would it be easy? No. But then again, neither is the life of many a Tibetan struggling to find their identity and cultural future in this world.

Chapter 1

Climbing for a Cause
August 11, 2002

Anyone who participates seriously in a sport soon learns the names and stories behind the athletes who set its standards of excellence. Those at the top become the mark, the model for those who are learning.

It didn't take long after I began climbing in the late 1970s for me to hear the name Galen Rowell. The stories told of a California auto mechanic who closed his repair shop, packed his camera and climbing gear, and headed for the mountains. His adventures became the stuff of legends, of stories told and retold around campfires in climbing camps everywhere. Before the grease had worn off his hands, he was climbing with the best climbers of Yosemite, completing visionary routes years ahead of their time. But that wasn't all; he was doing these extraordinary climbs and recording them with photographs that changed the nature of outdoor photography forever.

His eye for just the right angle, just the right lighting, quickly earned him assignments for magazines like *Outside, Backpacker, National Geographic* and *LIFE*. His photographs became illustrations in dozens of books, many of which he wrote himself.

He traveled on every continent and climbed in many of the major mountain ranges on earth. He visited the North Pole, the South Pole and was the climbing leader of the 1983 West Ridge Expedition on Mount Everest, but always he returned to the mountains he loved best, the Sierra Nevadas. There he hiked, ran and skied, searching for new rock faces to add to his long list of first ascents.

As I was learning to climb, Galen's photos inspired me to explore remote places. His books were insights into a lifestyle I valued. I wanted to explore valleys and glaciers, ridges and summits. Galen Rowell packed adventure into his life, and I wanted to do the same with mine.

Sometimes John Jancik gets obsessed with ideas. In fact, that is how I met him.

In 1989, Ken Zerbst, who worked for John's company, ECHO Geophysical Corporation in Denver, called me to ask for a reference for a climber who wanted to join a trip that Ken and John were organizing to northern Greenland. I answered the questions for the reference and asked several of my own. By the end of the conversation, Ken said, "You sound like you should be on this expedition, too."

Ken and John had been friends at the University of Wisconsin-Milwaukee in the late 1970s. During one geology class, they conceived the idea of going to northern Greenland and climbing there. Over the years, they had talked about the trip. They had attempted to organize it on more than one occasion, but it had never happened. Their plans for 1989 were to spend ten weeks in North Peary Land and climb several unnamed peaks. It sounded exciting, but the timing was wrong for me. I declined.

I thought about the trip and knew I had missed an exciting event. I did not know Ken or John, so I assumed they would go on the expedition, and I would never hear from them again.

Then, in 1995, I got another call from Ken. He asked if I remembered talking to him about the 1989 journey to Greenland.

I did.

He wanted to know if I was still interested in going to Greenland.

I was.

The timing was better for me, so I drove to Denver to meet John and Ken. We examined maps of northern Greenland and talked about their plans. It was an incredible idea, a chance to really explore a region that was largely unknown. It was an opportunity to climb peaks no one had touched, to cross glaciers no one had ever walked on, to see vistas no human eye had witnessed.

After I met John and Ken, I agreed to go, and we spent the winter making endless plans to organize the flights and equipment we would need to travel and climb in such a remote environment.

As we were making plans, one member of the team found out he had conflicts with work commitments and was forced to drop out. John and Ken wanted to replace him quickly so we could continue with the preparations. I immediately suggested that Joe Sears would be perfect. Joe, a Ph.D. research chemist from Kennewick, Washington, had been my college roommate, and we had been climbing together for fifteen years.

John and Ken talked with Joe, and soon, Joe was added to the roster.

While looking over Joe's paperwork, John discovered an interesting tidbit. He and Joe both shared May 19 as a birthday. "When I saw that," John said, "how could I not add him to the team?" It was the first of many common identities we would discover as we headed toward Greenland. By chance, it had also been May 19 when I drove to Denver to first meet John and Ken.

After a year of planning and training, we landed in a Twin Otter plane on the northern coast of Greenland. We unloaded our equipment and said goodbye to the pilot. He would come back for us in twenty-three days.

Our first goal was to walk across the sea ice to Oodaaq Island, the northernmost point of land on earth. After Oodaaq was four hundred miles of sea ice to the North Pole.

The team walked across the ice to Kaffeklubben Island, a prominent glacial moraine a mile north of the coast. From there, we scouted the sea ice for the lower and hidden rocks marking Oodaaq Island. We waded through icewater pools on top of the sea ice and found a small island, flooded by the meltwater, that we assumed was Oodaaq Island. Since the Danish group who discovered Oodaaq Island had flown there in a helicopter, we were the first group that ever walked to Oodaaq. Although we didn't know it at that moment, our sloshy hike to Oodaaq would give us a pleasant surprise in the future.

We had reached the island at midnight. In northern Greenland in July, the sun never sets for the full month. The permanent daylight is an explorer's dream, and we took full advantage of it. After reaching Oodaaq, we went back to the mainland, and over the next two weeks, we were able to climb several unnamed, unclimbed peaks, and eventually make the first ascent of the highest peak in the H.H. Bennedict Mountains: Star Spangled Banner Peak, named by the Danish.

When I joined the American Top of the World Expedition, I learned that one climber who had already signed up was Galen Rowell. I was excited to spend a month in Greenland with Galen and get to know him better. I wanted to learn more about his past expeditions, and about his photography and writing. I had many questions for him.

Galen told me he had seen the northern coast of Greenland from a Russian nuclear icebreaker during an expedition to the North Pole. He had been intrigued by the remoteness of the region and the lure of the northernmost land. He was interested in joining the American Top of the World expedition from the first time he heard about it.

Getting to know Galen on the expedition had been a treat. I watched him work his photography, and was thrilled to see his photos of our journey in *LIFE* magazine. At the time, however, we did not know how his participation in the 1996 American Top of the World Expedition would affect our lives over the next twenty years.

On that trip to Greenland, Joe and I became good friends with John and Terri. We talked about the possibility of doing other trips together: perhaps Granite Peak, the highest peak in Montana, or other fun adventures. We ended the trip with vague plans, but nothing definite rose out of those plans. A couple of years passed, and we talked occasionally. We all continued to climb and hike separately, but we didn't get back together as quickly as we hoped.

However, a year after the Greenland trip, John offered me a job as a seismic data marketer for his company, ECHO Geophysical Corporation in Denver. The position also included writing the corporate newsletter. I had been a high school English teacher for twenty years and still enjoyed what I was doing. I decided I did not want to leave teaching, but I proposed to John that I could write the newsletter from Montana. He liked the idea, so we met to discuss the guidelines for the newsletter.

He was adamant from the start that he did not want his newsletter to simply repeat the information from the marketing brochures. He wanted to focus on the people who made the company run. We named the newsletter SeisNOTES and over the next fourteen years, we published forty issues that contained stories about almost every employee who ever worked for ECHO Geophysical. We also wrote about many of our climbing and hiking trips. Features on interesting people. Accounts of adventure travels. It was the perfect writing assignment for me.

It was also a chance to work with John and continue talking about ideas for mountain climbing and adventure travel. Those discussions would form the basis for dozens of adventures throughout the next two decades.

Then, in 2000, the idea surfaced to go back to Greenland. The 1996 American Top of the World Expedition had been our best expedition. The unclimbed mountains and valleys, the glistening glaciers, the isolated nature of the travel, the endless daylight, had really captured our souls. So John, Terri, and Ken formed the 2001 Return to the Top of the World Expedition. Joe and I were included. Galen Rowell would not be able to return with us. In his place was another legend of the climbing world, Vernon Tejas, a professional mountain guide from Anchorage, Alaska. He had climbed the classic routes of the world, including the Seven Summits (the highest mountain on each of the seven continents), and reached the top of Alaska's Denali in the dead of winter—alone. He is usually off on another climb before his boots have dried from the previous adventure.

Vernon is perpetual motion incarnate. He can climb day after day and never lose his smile. If an expedition stalls because of weather or travel arrangements, he pulls out his fiddle or harmonica and soon has the entire team tapping their feet to his large repertoire of songs. He can sense when other people are happy, when they are concerned, and when they have crossed the limit of their comfort zone; he is the classic mountain guide.

Climbing with Galen Rowell in 1996 and Vernon Tejas in 2001 were two highlights of my mountaineering career. Both men have committed years of their lives to seeking adventures in the mountains of the world, and both have left their mark on the sport.

When we arrived a second time in North Peary Land, we had a question in mind. After we reached the island in the sea ice in 1996, we compared our GPS readings and photographs with those of the Danish group. There were some differences, most notably that the island we stood on was farther north. Had we discovered a new northernmost land on earth?

This question interested not only us but also the Danish Polar Center, the organization responsible for issuing permits to climb and explore in Greenland. John had exchanged emails, photographs, and notes with the Center's logistics officer, Hauge Anderson. By the time we left for Greenland, both our team and the Center suspected that Oodaaq Island might actually be multiple islands. There was one way to find out—fly over that region of the Arctic Ocean and compare all the GPS coordinates.

John arranged to have the pilot fly over Oodaaq on the way to dropping us off at Frigg's Fjord, where the 2001 expedition would begin. Andersson agreed to participate in the flyover and met the team in North Peary Land.

From the plane, the team could see the island we had discovered in 1996, but not the original Oodaaq. We learned that more than one island exists and that our island was the northernmost land on earth. We had made a discovery that changed a small piece of the geography of the world.

The 2001 Return to the Top of the World Expedition had a slightly different plan from the first Greenland trip. We wanted to climb

A Journey Supporting The Rowell Fund

Helvetia Tinde (Swiss Peak), the highest mountain in the northernmost range on earth, and the mountain that first captured the imagination of John and Ken during their geology class in the 1970s.

The mountain had been climbed by a British military group in 1969, and John Jancik had tracked down the leader of that expedition, Colonel John Peacock, who lived outside of London. The two exchanged phone calls and emails, and eventually Peacock gave Jancik a small British flag that he had carried up Helvetia Tinde durng the first ascent. We intended to take that flag back to the summit.

Five years to the day after we stood together on the summit of Star Spangled Banner Peak, John, Ken, Joe, and I, along with Vernon Tejas, raised the American flag, beside the British flag given to us by Colonel Peacock, on the summit of Helvetia Tinde. From that beautiful summit, we could see hundreds of peaks in the Roosevelt Mountains, Bennedict Mountains, Daly Mountains, and we could look out across an endless expanse of sea ice on the Arctic Ocean.

After the ascent of Hevetia Tinde, we hauled our sleds north to Sands Fjord. We camped on the sea ice and woke in the morning to begin our next goal, searching for the northernmost mountain on earth. It seemed like a fun project, but we didn't anticipate one of the biggest problems would be the question, "What is a mountain?"

Along the northern coast of Greenland, a line of mountains at 83 degrees north latitude faces the Arctic Ocean. One of those mountains is the planet's northernmost. After traversing the North Peary Land peninsula from south to north, we spent four days climbing and measuring fourteen summits in an attempt to locate the northernmost mountain. At least six of those peaks had never been climbed before.

The team took two GPS readings and two altimeter readings on every summit. We also measured the altitude of the saddles between connecting peaks. By the time we finished, we had collected pages of data about these mountains.

Why so much information? Why not look at a map, point to the northernmost mountain and go climb it? The problem is that there is no universal definition for what constitutes a mountain. How does a mountain differ from a hill, mound, or other similar feature? Also, what might be named a mountain in one geographic area might not qualify as a mountain in another area. What is a mountain in North Carolina might not get noticed in Colorado. A Colorado mountain would seem insignificant in Nepal or Tibet.

In the end, the highest peak in the massif east of Sands Fjord was our choice. It is a mountain with three small rock spires on its summit. We named it the Three-Toothed Mountain and christened it the Northernmost Mountain in the World, a distinction that probably has no significance for anyone beyond the group that was there that day. It had been an interesting search, and by climbing and measuring so many peaks, we were able to know that we had definitely stood on the northernmost mountain on earth.

After two expeditions to North Peary Land, Greenland, we had formed strong friendships and had many ideas about future trips. Having completed two journeys called The American Top of the World Expedition and the Return to the Top of the World Expedition, we decided we liked the "Top of" term and wanted to continue future trips using that as a theme for our group.

The first direct contact I had with Galen Rowell came in 1987 when I was writing a book about why climbers chose to participate in the sport. When I explained my project, he quickly agreed to help me. We couldn't arrange to meet, so I settled for a two-hour phone interview. As I expected, he offered a wealth of material for my book. When my book was published, I sent him a copy and received a warm letter in response.

By 2002, John and I had co-authored the book, *Under the Midnight Sun,* about the two Greenland expeditions. As it went to press, we received the news of Galen's death.

Galen and Barbara had made many trips to the Himalayas and had a special fondness for Tibet. They were deeply interested in the condition of the Tibetan people, who had long suffered since the invasion of Tibet by China in 1950. Galen had first visited Tibet in

1981, and many of his photos were of its people and its rich cultural heritage, as well as the dwindling animal populations.

In 1989, Galen and Barbara went to Dharamsala, India, the home of the Dalai Lama, and presented a slide show to him. He especially enjoyed the photos of the animals. After Galen and Barbara returned to California, Galen had an inspiration while hiking on the John Muir Trail. He wanted to create a book which featured his photos with the words of the Dalai Lama. The result, a book called *My Tibet*, was published in 1990.

When I heard about the plane crash, I found it hard to imagine that a man who had survived so many adventures in the most remote corners of the globe had died in his own backyard. I'm glad his photography will keep his achievements alive for future generations, so they may learn from him as I did.

Following the deaths of Galen and Barbara, the International Campaign for Tibet, a Washington, D.C., organization whose goals include monitoring the situation in Tibet and providing assistance to Tibetan people, created The Rowell Fund for Tibet in honor of Galen and Barbara Rowell and their passion for the people of Tibet.

The Rowell Fund for Tibet, launched in 2003, focuses on providing support for Tibetan photographers, filmmakers, writers, artists, and musicians. Its purpose is "to encourage and support the work of Tibetans in the language and visual arts who make significant contributions to society."

The Board of Directors of The Rowell Fund for Tibet is composed of many mountain climbers including Conrad Anker, Jimmy Chin, David Breashears, as well as 1996 Greenland teammates John Jancik, Terri Baker, and Bob Palais.

Being part of The Rowell Fund for Tibet inspired John to take action. In 2005, he called me and asked, "What if I tried to climb the highpoints of all 50 states and used that as a fundraiser for The Rowell Fund for Tibet? Is that a good idea?"

"It's a great idea. Can I help?"

He had decided to name the project 50 for Tibet. The second part of his idea shocked me. He said he wanted to complete all 50 state highpoints in one calendar year.

As part of the first climb made by the 50 for Tibet project, climbers traverse a snowfield on the ascent of Mount Whitney (14,505 feet), the highpoint of California.
Photo by John Jancik.

Chapter 2

The Top of the American Southwest
June 14, 2006

There are many state highpoints that are reached by driving a car to the spot, stepping out, taking a photo, and counting the highpoint done. States like Florida, Delaware, and Ohio fit that category. However, there are several states, especially in the west, that are significant mountaineering objectives. Mount Hood in Oregon, Mount Rainier in Washington, Granite Peak in Montana, Gannett Peak in Wyoming, and most notably Denali (Mount McKinley) in Alaska require specialized equipment and mountain training. Gannett Peak in Wyoming takes most of a week to climb, and Denali can take twenty-three to thirty days, depending on the snow conditions and the weather. The chance of failing and needing to return is a factor on any of the higher, more difficult peaks, so setting out to do these peaks in one year is, to say the least, ambitious. John is ambitious.

To promote 50 for Tibet, John designed a logo which featured a view of Mount Whitney, the highest peak in California and a mountain just outside Galen and Barbara's hometown. He created a brochure to promote 50 for Tibet and in it he wrote: "Barbara and Galen Rowell were friends of ours who inspired us to think globally and to understand that we all lose when other cultures and environments are destroyed. In their honor, our family has established 50 for Tibet, a private volunteer effort to promote the spirit and culture of Tibet by raising money for The Rowell Fund and awareness of the occupation of Tibet."

John said, "When Galen joined our 1996 American Top of the World Expedition, he represented more than just a world-class photographer and mountaineer. He was so much more; an articulate, well-read and energetic person. From that, I learned that being passionate about the things you care about was not a bad thing, as some people believe, but a character trait of successful individuals in life."

To use the 50 for Tibet project as a fundraiser, John contacted people he knew in the business world and asked them for contributions to The Rowell Fund for Tibet. Some people made direct contributions and others wanted to make pledges for each state highpoint reached. Interest in the project took off quickly, and John began the logistical work. He had to take into account the timing on many of the highpoints. The higher, mountaineering summits would need to be done in the summer months, while lower highpoints, particularly in the south, could easily be done in the winter.

One decision John made early was important to the success of the fundraising side. Few people want to donate to a project thinking that their money may be used to cover expenses like food, airline tickets, and rental cars. They want their dollars going to the core project. With that in mind, John committed his company, ECHO Geophysical Corporation, to cover all travel and other expenses related to the logistics and administration of the 50 for Tibet campaign. As John said, "One hundred percent of the donations will go directly to The Rowell Fund for Tibet."

John, who lives in Parker, Colorado, wanted to involve family, friends, employees, and clients in the project, especially in the pursuit of reaching the fifty state highpoints. Terri was instrumental in helping create the promotional ideas and plan the overall project. She participated in many of the highpoint trips, as did her son, David Baker, also an employee at ECHO Geophysical. Several other ECHO employees would participate in one or more of the highpointing trips, as would some of ECHO's clients. Joe Sears and I joined in as many 50 for Tibet events as our work schedules permitted.

This was a great opportunity to renew friendships and build

enthusiasm for future adventures. John, Terri, Joe, and I had been together in Greenland for the 1996 Top of the World Expedition. David Baker had joined the four of us and three others (Vernon Tejas, Ken Zerbst, Jim McCrain) for the 2001 Return to the Top of the World Expedition. Then, in 2002, all five of us—John, Terri, David, Joe and I, along with four other friends and family members (Sammy Sears, Romney Gardiner, Jim Schaefer, and Nichol Santilli) formed the Top of Africa Expedition to Mount Kilimanjaro in Tanzania.

As a continental highpoint, Kilimanjaro intrigued our group. We hired guides and porters, as required by Tanzanian law, and after six days of fascinating climbing, we left our high camp at midnight and climbed under a full moon to reach the 19,341-foot summit. We stood on top of Mount Kilimanjaro at six a.m. to watch the sun rise over the roof of Africa.

The climb had been a dream for many of us, but the real adventure developed on the descent. My 16-year-old daughter, Romney, had joined us on the trip and had climbed well, reaching the summit in fine style. However, on the trail down, she had vomited and become very weak. We spent that night in a tent with her being sick all night. In the morning, she was exhausted and unable to walk on her own. Four porters took turns, and in an amazing demonstration of strength and endurance, carried her piggyback off the mountain. As the team's doctor, Terri was concerned. Most mountain climbers get sick on the way up as the thinning atmosphere causes problems. Romney, on the other hand, was strong on the way up and weak on the way down. We spent a couple of days trying to solve her medical problems, before we realized that her illness had nothing to do with the mountain, high altitude, malaria, or food sickness—it was a congenital bowel obstruction. Even after we returned to town, her condition only grew worse.

After a frightening day in a questionable hospital, we ended up life-flighting her to Nairobi, Kenya, for abdominal surgery to save her life. John and Terri gave up their chance to go on a photo safari in the Serengeti National Park, flew with Romney and me to Nairobi, and stayed several days longer than planned in Africa. In the end, Romney's surgery went well, and she recovered, but there were days of strong fear and concern. While the 2002 Top of Africa Expedition was not part of the 50 for Tibet project, (which did not start until 2006) the emotional events with Romney in Africa helped us forge deep and lasting friendships which then created the basis for the teamwork and camaraderie necessary to make 50 for Tibet, with its infinite number of working parts, merge into the machine it eventually became.

It seemed appropriate to kick off the 50 for Tibet project with a dinner at Mountain Light Photography, Galen's photo gallery, in Bishop, California, on June 14, 2006. Galen's son, Tony Rowell, and daughter, Nicole Rowell Ryan, along with members of the Mountain Light staff, hosted the event.

Nicole said, "It seems fitting that a fund preserving the culture of Tibet would carry on my father's legacy. My grandfather, Edward Zbitovsky Rowell, started out as a theology major his first couple of years at the University of Chicago. He spent time as a student pastor and eventually became a Professor of Philosophy at UC Berkeley. He was very involved in the Unitarian Church in Berkeley. Surprisingly, with that strong religious background, I really never saw my father embrace a religious culture until he discovered Tibetan Buddhism. He was very moved by the people of Tibet and their whole culture as much as he was by their mountain regions. I believe he even wore a Tibetan shirt during his wedding to Barbara in 1981. So, to me, there is no better fitting tribute to his honor than to have a fund in his name preserving the culture of Tibet that he had come to love and respect so much. It is an honor to be part of this legacy."

Two groups of climbers attended the dinner. The first group included climbers who had donated money to The Rowell Fund for Tibet in order to have the chance to climb Mount Whitney, the highest peak in the forty-eight contiguous states, with legendary climbers Conrad Anker from Bozeman, Montana, and Peter Croft from Bishop, California. That group included Tony Rowell and John Ackerly, at that time the President of the International Campaign for Tibet, and others. Those thirteen climbers would be ascending The

Mountaineer's Route on Mount Whitney, a route on which Galen Rowell made the first ski descent in 1974.

The second group was our team of eleven. We would be climbing the standard trail from Whitney Portal, a twenty-two-mile hike, and we intended to climb it round-trip in one day. We also hoped that the two groups might be able to see each other at the summit of Mount Whitney.

The Mountaineer's Route group left the morning after the dinner and camped partway up Mount Whitney. Our group spent time in the afternoon on a snowfield near the highway to get some of the new climbers a little experience in walking on the slanting snow and in using an ice axe. We camped that night at Whitney Portal.

We got up at one-thirty a.m. and left the campsite an hour later. It is difficult to climb with so many climbers in each group because of the variety of technical backgrounds and fitness levels. Our group started out well and made good time, arriving at Outpost Camp in two hours. Beyond there, we hiked and watched the sunrise, lighting up the east face of Mount Whitney, a view much like the one John used to create the logo for 50 for Tibet.

There was much more snow than we expected, so when we arrived at Trail Camp and the start of the notorious switchbacks (one report told us there are ninety-nine switchbacks), we could not see any trail. We simply put on our crampons, pulled out our ice axes, and headed uphill. We reached the top of the snow at about ten a.m., but by then, the group was spread out below us on the snowfield. John and I waited half an hour, then began the hike along the summit ridge. That part of the hike is all above 13,800 feet, so it was slower walking and several sections were snow-covered.

We reached the 14,495-foot summit at noon, and as I was walking toward the stone hut at the highest point, I noticed a person walking to my left. I glanced at him, but he had a coat and helmet on, so I didn't realize for a few seconds that it was John Ackerly. We both started laughing. We had parted in Bishop two days before, but we had arrived at the summit of Mount Whitney at exactly the same time.

24   Highpointing for Tibet

*(Right) Jessica Morse and John Jancik on the summit of Mount Whitney, the highest point in the contiguous 48 states.
Photo courtesy of John Jancik.*

*(Below). Some of the members of the Mountaineers' Route Team on the summit of Mount Whitney. Climbers included Conrad Anker, Peter Croft and Tony Rowell.
Photo by Tony Rowell.*

Climbers followed each of us and soon, we had a crowd gathered on the summit. We were excited because 50 for Tibet now officially had one state highpoint accomplished. The Mountaineer's Route group were excited because many of the donors had reached the summit and had had a great experience. We enjoyed a friendly lunch, a lot of laughter, and a few quiet moments to think about Galen, Barbara, and the people of Tibet, before taking a long look at the peaks and valleys of the Sierra Nevada Mountains, the first of many beautiful views we would enjoy that summer.

With perfect conditions on the summit, we stayed almost two hours, before beginning the long descent. The snow on the switchbacks helped us out because we could slide down several sections of that, saving time, energy, and sore knees in the process. By late afternoon, we had been on the trail over twelve hours, and I could feel the tiredness settle in. We took a couple of rest breaks, refilled water bottles, and tried to keep our outlook happy. One step after another. Climbing can be very exciting at times, but there are also many hours of tedious pacing, of moving bodies and equipment over large tracts of terrain, in order to enjoy the moments of accomplishment. The final five hours of walking down that trail, seemed numb, like my legs were moving ahead on autopilot.

Terri Baker's daughter, Jessica Morse from Morrison, Colorado, said that during the ascent, she had serious doubts about whether she might reach the top, but the summit "was beautiful, and I was so happy, and I thought the hard part was over. Wrong! The hike down was excruciatingly long, and I was completely exhausted. When I finally finished, I remember questioning why in the world anyone ever willingly chooses to do this sort of thing and actually enjoys it. That thought obviously didn't stick around the next time I was asked to climb."

We reached our car at seven thirty p.m., seventeen hours after we started for the summit. There is a certain glow that fills a mountaineer at the end of a long day. It is a combination of exhaustion, of relief, of satisfaction, in having pushed hard enough to overcome the obstacles of a mountain, but more importantly, of overcoming obstacles inside the mind and heart. Our long day on Mount Whitney left us weary, but proud.

From California we drove to Nevada, stopping along the highway to watch a herd of wild horses walking across the desert. Boundary Peak, the highpoint of Nevada, is a dry mountain, covered in dust and loose scree baking under the desert sun. We were surprised to find one thin snow gulley running five hundred feet up the mountain, giving us good footing and an easy ascent, but it ran out too quickly, and we were forced onto more floundering scree. While it is not a technically difficult peak, the loose footing and the fact that it came two days after we had exhausted ourselves on Mount Whitney made it seem much more difficult than we expected. We had trained hard before starting the 50 for Tibet climbs, but we didn't really have our mountain legs under us yet and hadn't fully recovered.

Boundary Peak gets its name from its location so close to the state line between California and Nevada. One feature that is interesting is that Boundary Peak is actually a subpeak of Montgomery Peak which is in California, but is four hundred feet taller than Boundary Peak. It seemed strange to be on a state highpoint yet be overshadowed by a taller peak so near. At 13,143 feet, Boundary Peak gave us views of pastel tones far into the desert distance.

We drove south to Las Vegas, then east to Flagstaff, Arizona, The highpoint of Arizona is Humphreys Peak (12,633 feet), an extinct volcano, which outlines the northern skyline of Flagstaff. The trail took us through the Arizona Snow Bowl ski area and into lush forests, a sharp contrast to the previous travels in the desert. Several switchbacks brought us to the Agassiz Saddle between Humphreys Peak and Mount Agassiz. Above the saddle, the trail was rocky, and we crossed three false summits before arriving at the true summit. We spent only two minutes on the peak, because swarms of yellowjackets were everywhere. With the full-panorama view, we could see smoke from forest fires that would spread, closing the mountain and its hiking trails only two days after our ascent.

On our rest day, we drove to Taos, New Mexico, and camped near the trailhead for Wheeler Peak. We chose the Williams Lake route, which begins with a gentle flat mile of trail to the lake followed by over 4,000 vertical feet of very abrupt rise to the summit. This upper section was a grassy slope on stair-step ground, making it easy to

A Journey Supporting The Rowell Fund

move up the high-angle terrain. At the top of the slope, the summit ridge was an easy walk. We paused to look into a large valley east of the peak where fog had settled in far below us. Another glorious day of weather let us relax and enjoy the views from the 13,161-foot summit. With our first four highpoints finished, we drove home to spend a week with our families and jobs.

As part of the 50 for Tibet project, John had two unique and fun ideas to provide a sense of continuity throughout the state highpoints. He had purchased an American flag when we went to Greenland in 1996. We had photographed the flag on the Top of the World Island, Star Spangled Banner Peak, and other mountains, and then had brought the same flag back to Greenland in 2001 for photos on Helvetia Tinde and the peaks involved in the search for the northernmost mountain on earth. John had also made a 50 for Tibet flag. He wanted to take photos on each summit displaying both of the flags. He also had an autographed copy of Galen Rowell's book *Mountains of the Middle Kingdom*. We decided it would be fun to sign the book on each summit. Any of our own climbers who were there could sign it, as could any other climbers we happened to meet at each summit. It would be a good way to meet other people, as well as share information about the project.

We also noticed that the "Top of" theme we had created with the Top of the World expedition and the Top of Africa expedition could apply to everything we were doing with 50 for Tibet. With that in mind, we realized that we had already accomplished the Top of California, Top of Nevada, Top of New Mexico, and Top of Arizona climbing trips. Next up would be the Top of New England.

After the Rowell Fund for Tibet started in 2003, it was able to give $37,240 to twelve Tibetans, most based in India, but several in Tibet, the U.S. and the U.K. In its second year, the Fund supported eleven projects and provided nearly $50,000 in grants. We hoped our efforts through the 50 for Tibet project would result in donations that would allow The Rowell Fund to increase their grants.

Steve Gardiner is buffeted by the wind on the exposed upper ridge on Mount Katahdin in Maine. The heavy clouds in the background brought rain and poor visibility throughout the climb.
Photo by John Jancik.

Chapter 3

The Top of New England
July 1, 2006

As we began our climbs for 50 for Tibet, I think each of us had certain peaks that appealed to us for a variety of reasons. One peak that captured my imagination was Mount Katahdin, the highpoint of Maine. I knew one of my favorite writers, Henry David Thoreau, had climbed it in September 1846, and I had read his essay about the ascent. In fact, I reread it on the flight to Boston. Partly my interest in Katahdin was to walk in Thoreau's footsteps, but I had also seen pictures of the mountain and read other accounts. It sounded like a peak we would really enjoy.

After we landed in Boston, we drove north to Brunswick, Maine, to visit Bowdoin College and see the Peary Arctic Museum. After our two trips to the northern coast of Greenland, we were interested in information about the region and the history of polar exploration. Inside the museum, we got to see many of Robert Peary's exploration artifacts and learn about his extensive Arctic travels. We remembered our own journeys in that region and commented that we had landed there in a Twin Otter airplane. Peary and Matthew Henson had reached the northern coast of Greenland by dogsled. We gained respect for what they had done in the early 1900s.

Our climb on Katahdin began early. We were up at four a.m. and arrived at the gate to Baxter State Park at four forty-five. We checked in, got through the gate at five thirty and started the hike at six. The fog was thick, so our visibility was limited. No sweeping views of the Maine woods that Thoreau described, but we did notice how dense the forest was on each side of the narrow trail. Without the trail, it would be difficult or impossible to make any progress up the mountain.

When we climbed high enough to leave the forest, we scrambled up a rocky ridge. It was fun climbing and the thick fog gave a sense of mystery. We could see perhaps twenty feet up the ridge above us, and the stones faded into fog.

In his essay "Ktaadn," Thoreau described a similar scene. His climbing companions had stopped, deciding they would pick mountain cranberries. Thoreau pressed on toward the summit, climbing "alone over huge rocks, loosely poised, a mile or more, still edging toward the clouds—for though the day was clear elsewhere, the summit was concealed by mist." As he climbed, those rocks spread out endlessly in front of him. He saw in them the "random patterns of nature, the forces of nature that would, over time, move those rocks around on the mountain, or down into the smiling and verdant plains and valleys of earth. This was an undone extremity of the globe."

At one point on the ridge, we paused when another group of climbers quickly caught up with us and passed us. They were moving easily up the steep ridge. We visited with them for a few minutes and learned that they were thru-hikers on the Appalachian Trail. The summit of Katahdin is generally considered the northern terminus of the Appalachian Trail, so it was exciting for us to see them finish their hike. The three hikers had all started out individually and after seeing each other several times at the campsites, they formed a group. One man told me he was sixty-one and had just retired as a Dupont engineer. Another man was about thirty and the woman was about twenty-five. Their many months of hiking had left them very fit and after talking with us briefly, they moved on past us toward their final goal.

A Journey Supporting The Rowell Fund

"Mount Katahdin was a wonderful climb," John said. "We started the hike in sunshine and in a beautiful forest and summited in dense fog above timberline. The variety of weather we experienced that day surely added to the experience. Everything from thunderstorms to dense fog to sunshine. The route itself was also fun with a bit of rock climbing added to the trek."

We passed a point on the mountain called Thoreau Springs and continued on to the summit at about ten thirty. We were still in heavy fog and had not seen a view of the area yet. It was windy and chilly on the summit, so we stayed only about ten minutes, then left. Some five hundred feet below the summit, the fog broke open, and we had great views down onto the forest and lakes below. We walked for two hours with fine views of the area before the clouds moved in

David Baker with the summit sign on Maine's Mount Katahdin (5,267 feet), the northern terminus of the Appalachian Trail. Moments earlier, the team met three hikers finishing a months-long trek on the famous trail.
Photo by John Jancik.

again. It rained on us the remainder of the descent, and we arrived at our car at three p.m.

Our moments on the summit of Katahdin had been very similar to what Thoreau experienced one hundred sixty years before. When he "reached the summit of the ridge, which those who have seen in clearer weather say is about five miles long, and contains a thousand acres of table-land, I was deep within the hostile ranks of clouds, and all objects were obscured by them." Occasionally, the wind blew the clouds enough that he could see glimpses of the forest and valley below or views of the rocky slopes surrounding him, but mostly he felt like he was "sitting in a chimney and waiting for the smoke to blow away."

We drove in to Millinocket to find our hotel and stopped at a convenience store for a drink. Inside we met the three thru-hikers, who were very excited about hiking 2,190 miles of the Appalachian Trail from Springer Mountain, Georgia, to Mount Katahdin in Maine, a route that crosses fourteen states. Their sense of joy in their accomplishment was irresistible. Even though we were in the midst of our own long-term project, I found myself wondering what it would feel like to walk the full Appalachian Trail in one season. Perhaps it would be a future project. One dream often sets up another.

The Top of New England trip also included Mount Washington in New Hampshire. There is a paved road to the summit, but the day we arrived it was closed. Mount Washington is known for its extremely high winds and that day, the wind was blowing sixty-five miles an hour, with gusts up to ninety-nine. We had talked about driving up the road, just for the unique experience of doing that, but we still intended to hike on the following day. Since winds of over two hundred miles an hour have been recorded on Mount Washington, we were concerned that our hike the next day may be in jeopardy.

I had long wanted to climb the trail up Tuckerman's Ravine, so we drove to Pinkham Notch to find the trailhead and a campground.

We were up and on the trail by five a.m. There was plenty of light to see as we hiked to Hermit Lakes, up 1,800 feet, by six fifteen. The

A Journey Supporting The Rowell Fund 33

morning was calm and clear, so we set out up the steep headwall of Tuckerman's Ravine. We passed several waterfalls and just below the top, we met our first wind. It was light, but we finished the steep headwall, and as we stepped onto the asphalt parking lot on top, the wind hit us at fifty mph, according to the weather station at the 6,289-foot summit.

We were debating about whether to hike back down, when a lady from England stopped and asked if we wanted a ride. We got in, and as we were going down the road, she told us she had been working in the area, but was leaving to go climb Mount Kilimanjaro. We told her our story of Kilimanjaro and wished her luck on her climb.

We celebrated July 4 with an easy walk up Mount Mansfield (4,393 feet), the highpoint of Vermont, followed in the afternoon by a visit to Ben and Jerry's Ice Cream Factory. We let the ice cream settle with a ferry ride across Lake Champlain and a drive into Lake Placid, New York, where we visited the Olympic Ice Rink, site of the U.S. Hockey Team's Miracle on Ice during the 1980 Winter Olympics.

The next morning we hiked up Mount Marcy, the highpoint of New York. It is not as steep as Mount Katahdin, but requires a fifteen-mile hike through the Adirondacks. Clouds moved in and out throughout the morning, but we were able to have good views of the surrounding mountains. Again, we had started early, so we were down from the climb by one thirty, which gave us time to visit Mount Van Hoevenberg, the site of the Olympic bobsled races. In the summer, they run bobsleds on wheels, so we bought tickets. What a change from our measured pace of hiking and climbing to spend a brief moment screaming down the bobsled run with a trained driver and brakeman.

The Top of New England trip needed a great finish--three state summits in one day. From Lake Placid we drove south through Albany and into the northwestern corner of Massachusetts, where we entered Mount Greylock State Reservation. Mount Greylock, at 3,489 feet, offers nice views of the surrounding Berkshire Mountains. A paved road leads to the summit where the ninety-three-foot high

Massachusetts Veterans War Memorial Tower resides. Although our 50 for Tibet project was designed to seek out the highest natural point in each state, we did climb the stairs to the top of the Tower for an even better view of the area.

From Mount Greylock, we drove south to the border with Connecticut, to locate Mount Frissell (2,454 feet). This is an interesting state highpoint because the Connecticut highpoint is on the southern side of Mount Frissell, but the summit of the mountain is actually higher and farther north in Massachusetts. Although most state highpoints are the top of a mountain or hill, Connecticut is an example where it is not. We hiked a couple of miles up the trail and found the trailside marker for the state highpoint, then continued north into Massachusetts to reach the summit of Mount Frissell. At the summit was a register for hikers to sign. In the notes in the register, we found the name of Gary Roach, a climber we were all familiar with because he had recently published a climber's guide to the mountains of Colorado.

Just after crossing the Rhode Island state line, we saw a sign on the side of the highway announcing that we were at the state highpoint. That sign is not accurate, because the exact highpoint, Jerimoth Hill, is a short walk off the highway. Though it is only eight hundred and twelve feet above sea level, this state highpoint had been a difficult one for many years. It was located on private land and the landowner did not want anyone on his property. He had posted signs and set up a security system to warn him if anyone trespassed. Fortunately for us, another family purchased the land in 2005, the year before we visited, and they had opened the short trail to the public. Because it had only recently been opened, the trail into the trees was not clearly marked. We were standing on the side of the highway considering what might be our path to the highpoint, when a man yelled to us. He was the new landowner, and he showed us where the trail was, visited with us for several minutes, and even signed the Galen Rowell book we were carrying to each highpoint. Since our visit to Jerimoth Hill, it has become the property of the state of Rhode Island and is open to visitors every day.

It had been a busy day, between Mount Greylock, Mount Frissell,

A Journey Supporting The Rowell Fund

and Jerimoth Hill. A highpointer's hat trick.

The day ended with us driving into Boston. The next day would be a free day before our flights home. John has long been a fan of John F. Kennedy, and he wanted to visit the JFK Museum. I had attended a summer seminar at Harvard University in 1989, so I wanted to walk through campus and revisit some of the sites from my earlier experience, and we wanted to take a whale-watching boat ride. Our highpointing efforts weren't only about reaching state summits.

We also spent some time talking about and reflecting on the overall organization of the 50 for Tibet project and how it might help The Rowell Fund assist people in Tibet and India.

Landlocked high in the Himalayan mountains, Tibet is a county that has a long history of isolation from the rest of the world. Humans have lived in the Tibet region for as much as 20,000 years, according to some reports, and the borders of Tibet have expanded and contracted, depending on who was ruling Tibet and what events were taking place in surrounding regions.

In about 640 AD, Songtsan Gampo unified several regions into the single country of Tibet. The succession of kings that followed supported Buddhism as the state religion. By the seventeenth century, the tradition of a theocratic government, headed by the Dalai Lama or his regents, controlled the country. The Dalai Lamas, believed to be incarnations of Chenrezig, the Bodhisattva of Compassion, have been the political and spiritual leaders of the Tibetan people, officially beginning with the fifth Dalai Lama in 1642.

That tradition, with a few exceptions, continued until 1959. The thirteenth Dalai Lama (the first was born in 1391), took power in 1895 and during his leadership, he briefly fled Tibet during a 1910 Chinese invasion but returned in 1912 to declare a complete independence from China and create a Tibetan flag, currency, and passports. He made extensive efforts to modernize Tibet by updating many laws, establishing foreign relations with other countries, and bringing electricity to Lhasa. He ruled Tibet until his death in 1933.

The fourteenth Dalai Lama was born July 6, 1935, in the village of Takster in the province of Amdo. Tradition in Tibet dictated that the regents, who controlled the country after the thirteenth Dalai Lama's death, would wait two years, then follow significant signs that would direct them to find the reincarnation in the form of a young boy.

While the thirteenth Dalai Lama was lying in state, his head reportedly turned from facing south to facing northeast. Not long after, the Regent was gazing into the water of a lake and saw a vision of three letters and a three-storied monastery with a turquoise and gold roof. He took the letters as a guide and with his assistants, headed toward Amdo where he found a monastery much like he had seen in his vision. After searching in nearby villages, the party discovered a boy who fit many other parts of the visions. The boy, upon seeing the Regent said, "Sera Lama," correctly identifying the monastery where the Regent lived. They watched the boy, without letting his parents know who they were. Soon they were convinced they had found the next Dalai Lama. They returned a few days later with several personal items from the thirteenth Dalai Lama and other items not related to the previous leader.

When they showed the boy the items, he correctly identified the items belonging to the thirteenth Dalai Lama, reportedly saying, "It's mine. It's mine." The boy, named Lhamo Thondrup (sometimes spelled Dhondrup), which means "Wish Fulfilling Goddess," was identified as the new Dalai Lama.

After a brief stay at Kumbum Monastery, Lhamo Thondrup and his party made the three-month journey to Lhasa where he was taken to live at the Norbulinka, the summer residence of the Dalai Lama. In the winter of 1940, he was taken to the Potala Palace, where he was installed as the spiritual leader of Tibet. During that ceremony, he gave up his birth name and assumed the name of Jamphel Ngawang Lobsang Yeshe Tenzin Gyatso.

To prepare him for his life as a leader, his tutors gave him intense lessons in history, Buddhist philosophy, medicine, Tibetan art and culture, and other subjects. His development went well as he seemed to be a perceptive student. This proved to be important, because by the time he was fifteen, China had made threatening gestures toward

A Journey Supporting The Rowell Fund

Tibet and rumors of Chinese troops crossing the border into Tibet were circling in Lhasa.

With these developments, the Regent requested that the Dalai Lama be named political leader earlier than expected. The proposal was approved and on November 17, 1950, the fourteenth Dalai Lama found himself the teenage leader of six million people on the verge of war with China. The Dalai Lama sent out requests for support to Great Britain and America, but received no encouraging news from either country.

Over the next years, tensions increased and in late 1954, the Dalai Lama traveled to China to talk with Mao Zadong and other Chinese leaders, with little progress. Over the next two or three years, more reports of Chinese abuse of Tibetan citizens reached the Dalai Lama until in March 1959, after the brutal retaliation by the Chinese toward the Tibetan uprising of March 10, it became clear that he must leave Lhasa or risk being captured or killed by the Chinese.

On March 17, he disguised himself as a soldier and walked through the crowds of people to the Kiychu River, where he met his assistants and family members. The group spent three weeks traveling through the high altitude and rugged terrain of Tibet. They journeyed mostly at night to avoid Chinese sentries and continued to the Indian border where they crossed into safety.

The Dalai Lama eventually set up a Tibetan government in exile in Dharamsala in northern India, where he lives to this day. He has become a world traveler, often visiting many countries each year, always speaking of the plight of the Tibetan people living in Tibet under Chinese occupation. In the beginning, he hoped to bring about freedom for Tibet, but has for many years asked for Tibetan autonomy within China, an approach he calls the Middle Way.

In his book *Mountains of the Middle Kingdom*, Galen Rowell outlines the challenge. "The Dalai Lama, no longer the naive teenager who fled Lhasa in 1951, has become one of the world's most astute political observers, well aware of the sad reality that no country in the modern world, whether subjugated or totally free, has ever successfully reverted to a past society, much less a theocracy.

He and his representatives have simply declared that he will only return to an independent Tibet."

His travels have turned him into an international celebrity, a popular speaker, and a figure of importance in world politics. He has met with world religious figures, scientists, philosophers, and political leaders to discuss the state and future of the world. He has received awards and honors from many nations and several honorary doctorates from universities.

In September 1987, he spoke to the U.S. Congress in Washington, DC, and proposed a Five Point Peace Plan for Tibet to deal with the terrible conditions experienced by those people who have remained in his homeland. In that speech, he proposed:

1. Transformation of the whole of Tibet into a zone of peace.

2. Abandonment of China's population transfer policy that threatens the very existence of the Tibetans as a people.

3. Respect for the Tibetan people's fundamental human rights and democratic freedoms.

4. Restoration and protection of Tibet's natural environment and the abandonment of China's use of Tibet for the production of nuclear weapons and dumping of nuclear waste.

5. Commencement of earnest negotiations on the future status of Tibet and of relations between the Tibetan and Chinese peoples.

Because of his non-violent opposition to the Chinese and his encouragement of a peaceful settlement to the Tibetan issue, the Dalai Lama received the Nobel Peace Prize in 1989.

In his eloquent style, the Dalai Lama, in his Nobel acceptance speech, said, "I accept the prize with profound gratitude on behalf of the oppressed everywhere and for all those who struggle for freedom and work for world peace. I accept it as a tribute to the man who founded the modern tradition of nonviolent action for change—Mahatma Gandhi—whose life taught and inspired me. And, of course, I accept it on behalf of the six million Tibetan people, my brave countrymen and women inside Tibet, who have suffered and continue to suffer so much. They confront a calculated and systematic strategy aimed at the destruction of their national and cultural identities. The prize reaffirms our conviction that with truth, courage and determination as our weapons, Tibet will be liberated."

Because the Dalai Lama is now eighty-two years old, there has been much speculation about his own reincarnation. Some Chinese authorities have said that since Tibet is part of China, a Chinese delegation will determine the Dalai Lama's successor. The Dalai Lama has said he will consult with Tibetan officials to determine if he should be reincarnated and if there should be a fifteenth Dalai Lama. He has said that if he chooses to be reincarnated, he will do so outside of Tibet and any other country controlled by China. He will only reincarnate in a free country and will leave clear, written instructions about his reincarnation. He warns that "no recognition or acceptance should be given to a candidate chosen for political ends by anyone, including those in the People's Republic of China."

The Top of New England trip was our third major trip of the summer. We were tired, but very happy that in a few short weeks, we had had summit success. We also seemed to be hitting the weather and other obstacles perfectly. We had reached the summits of Humphreys in Arizona and Wheeler in New Mexico just two days before forest fires shut down access to both peaks. We climbed Mount Katahdin a day after heavy rain washed over the peak. We climbed Mount Washington one day after extreme winds closed the road and any approaches to the mountain. We had attempted eleven highpoints and been successful on every one. We could only hope our good luck continued, especially since we were going to focus our next efforts on major mountaineering peaks in the Pacific Northwest and Rocky Mountains.

Joe Sears greets the sunrise at Disappointment Cleaver on Mount Rainier, the highpoint of the state of Washington.
Photo by John Jancik.

Chapter 4

The Top of the Northwest
July 17, 2006

As we headed toward the Pacific Northwest and the climbs of Mount Hood and Mount Rainier, we were excited to know that Tony Rowell, Galen's son, would be joining us for Mount Hood. Tony, who lives in Bishop, California, had climbed Mount Whitney with the group on the Mountaineer's Route, so we had already seen him on one summit of the 50 for Tibet project. It would be fun to have him along throughout the entire route on Mount Hood.

I was also looking forward to Joe Sears climbing with us. He had been with our group on both of the Greenland expeditions as well as the Top of Africa climb. In addition, he and I had climbed together in the Tetons and at Devils Tower, gone ice climbing on several frozen waterfalls, and spent a summer canoeing and backpacking in the Boundary Waters Canoe Area in Minnesota and Quetico Provincial Park in Ontario, Canada. Work duties had prevented him from joining us earlier in the summer, but he would be a valuable addition as we moved into the more technical peaks. Joe and I had the most climbing experience of the group, so it was nice to have the two of us together when we needed to make decisions about how to approach a climbing route, or to make sure that our safety concerns were met. By this point, Joe and I had been climbing together for almost thirty years. Our confidence in each other on a mountain was strong.

We drove from Portland to the Timberline Lodge campground on Mount Hood. Throughout the summer, we had developed a tradition of sleeping out on the ground. We hadn't pitched a tent in California, Maine, New Hampshire, New York, or Oregon. We were enjoying sleeping under the stars, and it was one less thing to deal with, especially when we left very early for a climb. On Mount Hood, we packed our backpacks and went to bed at nine p.m. We were up at one a.m.

We left the trailhead at two a.m. The main route up Mount Hood goes up the year-round ski slope on groomed snow. It made for easy walking, and we advanced to the top of the ski slope where we took a break from the wind, put on our crampons, and pulled out our ice axes. After some of the easier hiking peaks, it felt good to be on a true mountaineering route, and I could sense the excitement among the other climbers.

From the top of the ski run, the wind-packed snow was solid and offered good footing. We moved steadily upward toward the base of the Hogsback Ridge, the standard route on the mountain. We had heard that the upper part of the Hogsback Ridge, a series of rock towers known as the Pearly Gates, was not in good shape. We knew there were options, so we decided we would examine the route when we reached the bottom of the Hogsback Ridge.

On the flat area below the ridge, we could see a wide bergshrund, a gap between the upper part of the glacier and the snowfield above. That gap looked shattered, and the gulley between the rock towers above was filled with rotten rock. It looked too dangerous. As we talked it over, a solo climber coming down approached us. He said he had just climbed a route a bit farther west called the Mazama or Old Chutes route, and the route was in excellent condition. That changed our plans.

We traversed west to the base of the steep snow of the Mazama route. The snow conditions looked exceptional. The bootprints in the snow from where others had climbed before us marked where we needed to go. The sky was clear, and we were all feeling strong, so finding this route, in so much better condition than the Hogsback

Ridge, increased our excitement. Advancing onto the high-angle snow, we settled into a steady rhythm. Holding our ice axes in our uphill hands gave us good balance, and the crampons on our boots provided solid foot placements.

Progress was much slower as we climbed the steep section for four hundred vertical feet. Each step required more energy, more balance, more concentration, but after seeing how badly broken the upper section of the Hogsback Ridge was, we were happy to be struggling up the solid snow of the Mazama Route.

The four hundred-foot section was enough to get us around the problems we saw on the Hogsback Ridge, so we then turned east. The angle of the mountain eased back, and we soon arrived at the point above the Pearly Gates where we had initially intended to climb. I had climbed up the Hogsback Route and through the Pearly Gates in 1981 with my wife Peggy, just a few weeks after our wedding. As I approached the summit of Mount Hood for a second time, I remembered walking with her and the excitement we shared on reaching this beautiful summit.

The 50 for Tibet team reached the 11,239-foot top about nine-thirty am. Under the cloudless sky, we had views in all directions. Mount Rainier, one hundred and five miles to the north, dominated the skyline. We knew that Washington giant was our next goal. We also had a fine view of Mount Jefferson to the south.

Tony Rowell was smiling as he walked onto the summit. This was our twelfth summit in the 50 for Tibet project, designed to support The Rowell Fund for Tibet. He was pleased with both the climb and the way the project, in honor of his father and stepmother, was developing. He laughed as we unrolled the American flag and the 50 for Tibet flag and took our traditional photos. He was also quick to sign the copy of his father's book we were carrying. Tony had continued his father's interest in outdoor photography, specializing in night sky panoramas. On the summit of Mount Hood, he was busy with his camera for the forty-five minutes we stayed on top.

"Having Tony along on Mount Hood in Oregon definitely added to the whole significance and experience of the climb," John said. "I will never forget Tony's passion for taking photographs during the ascent. His image of the shadow of Mount Hood at sunrise is spectacular. Being Galen's son, Tony lives in the shadow of his dad's climbing and photography accomplishments. However, Tony did just fine during the climb and is an accomplished photographer in his own right. It was a real pleasure having him along with us."

One of the reasons climbers leave early in the morning, as we had done on Mount Hood, is that the midday sun often makes snowfields slushy. Even though we were early, we found our descent even slower than the ascent. Our boots sunk into the snow, making each step a challenge. It became an exhausting process, and we did not get back to our car until three p.m.

The next morning we dropped Tony at the airport in Portland and headed to Seaside, Oregon, for a much-needed day of rest. We

Joe Sears, John Jancik, David Baker, Jen Pauley, and Tony Rowell on the summit of Mount Hood, Oregon's highest point. Early explorers of the region placed the elevation of the mountain at over 18,000 feet.
Photo by Steve Gardiner.

strolled on the beach, waded in the surf, and swam in the ocean. At one point, David Baker and I were swimming, and I noticed that I was farther from the shore than I had been. I started swimming in, but felt like I was going nowhere. David said the same, and we soon realized we were caught in a riptide, a strong turbulent flow of water, pushing us straight out to sea. We swam farther north, out of the line of the riptide and were able to return to shore easily. As we walked up onto the beach, we discovered that the lifeguards had moved closer to us and were watching our progress.

"Did you get the gist of that riptide?" one asked as we left the water. Yes, we got it.

On July 21, we checked in with the rangers at Mount Rainier National Park. Climbing permits in hand, we set out for Camp Muir, the traditional camping spot at 10,080 feet. The day was sunny and warm. Perhaps it was the heat, or the climb on Mount Hood two days previous, or a long summer of traveling and climbing, but I felt like I dragged up the slope to Camp Muir. I moved slower than usual, and Joe told me he felt tired, too. In any case, the hike to Camp Muir is significant. It covers almost five miles, but more importantly for climbers with heavy backpacks, it gains 4,680 vertical feet.

We reached Camp Muir at three thirty and the stone hut, which holds long bunks that are available for climbers on a first-come basis. We had carried tents up with us, but the hut was open, so we moved inside and claimed bunk space for all five of us. After we ate dinner, a climbing ranger stopped by to talk with us. He explained that a large crevasse had opened on the mountain at about the 13,000-foot level. It was wide, stretching across a broad swath of the mountain, and was spanned by a single, narrow snow bridge. The ranger warned that the bridge was deteriorating in the intense summer sun, and cautioned us to be careful as we approached it. He added that if the bridge melted or collapsed, we might find it difficult or impossible to make the climb to the summit.

His comments worried me. I would have to climb across that thin snow bridge first and set up the anchor on the upper side for the others. I tried to imagine what it would look like and how it would affect us as we approached it and crossed it. I had been tired on the climb up to Camp Muir, but the ranger's comments had wakened me. I laid on the bunk, thinking about the possibilities that would face us in the morning. Would we safely cross the snow bridge? Would we have to search for a way around the crevasse? Would we have to turn back?

I remembered my first encounter with Mount Rainier. In 1979, a group of eight of us traveled from Wyoming in early June. We had made the climb up to Camp Muir with no trouble, but the next day, just as we reached the crater rim, a storm came over the mountain from the west and dropped a blizzard on us. We staggered down the mountain, searching in the blinding snow for the descent route. We were forced to stop and dig caves into the hard snow on the side of the mountain. We waited inside the caves for three hours for the blizzard to stop, before we could continue back to Camp Muir. It was a frightening experience, but everyone returned safe and healthy.

That experience haunted me for a few years after. If I were on a mountain and a storm was approaching, I could feel a knot in my stomach. I backed off a few mountains in threatening storms, and decided the best thing I could do would be to go back to Mount Rainier and climb it again, hopefully in better weather.

That chance came in 1994 when I went to Mount Rainier with Joe Sears and his brother-in-law Jim Bolster from New York City. We met in the campground near the base of Mount Rainier and the next day, climbed to Camp Muir. The following morning, we easily climbed to the summit under clear skies. It had taken fifteen years for me to get back to that mountain and erase some of the images of fear that lingered with it, but the return trip was what I needed.

As I lay in the stone hut at Camp Muir, thinking about the ranger's comments on the large crevasse with the tiny snow bridge, it was interesting to think about coming back to the same mountain for a third time another dozen years later. We had discussed this at the beginning of the 50 for Tibet project. I, and others, had already climbed some of the state highpoints before, as part of previous

A Journey Supporting The Rowell Fund 47

mountaineering adventures. We decided that those did not count for the 50 for Tibet project. We would only count peaks that were done during the time period of 50 for Tibet. I was fine with that. Mount Rainier is a mountain worthy of climbing more than once.

I may have slept some that night, but not much. We got up at one a.m. on July 22 and were climbing by two. We moved onto the Cowlitz Glacier and could see headlamps ahead of us. More than one party had already started. Moving through the dark with only the light from a headlamp is an eerie experience. We could see large blocks of ice that had broken off the glacier and tumbled into the large basin in the center. We proceeded carefully and cautiously.

Using our ice axes and crampons for safety, we moved into an area called Cadaver Gap. It was filled with snow, a gift for us because it was much easier walking than if we were on the loose rocks beneath the snow. As we reached the top of the Gap, we got to watch a magnificent sunrise. The first rays of light highlighted the horizon, then the rocky ridges and glaciers around and above us. We paused to eat, drink, and enjoy that moment. The light would mean we could see our steps better and would soon give us a warmer air temperature. Both would be welcome and would help us climb easier and faster.

Above Cadaver Gap, we hiked onto the Ingraham Glacier. Then we climbed past Disappointment Cleaver, where the angle of the snow increased, and we ran into the crevasses the ranger talked about. We tied everyone in our group to a rope so we could protect each other as we moved through the broken ice in the area. The first crevasses were small and easy to walk around. A short while later, some 1,400 feet below the crater rim, we came to the critical crevasse, the one with the narrow snow bridge.

As we approached the snow bridge, Joe said his mind was filled with questions. *Is it going to hold or is it going to break? How many people have been across this long narrow strip of snow this morning? Is our group going to be the one that breaks the snow bridge and completes the opening of the crevasse? Everyone else has made it across without incident, so why shouldn't we?*

There are several guide services that take climbers up Mount

Rainier. One of the guides had used snow pickets above and below the crevasse to fix a rope in place, a wise safety move.

When I got to the edge of the crevasse, I could see the small snow bridge. I would need to climb down four or five feet into the crevasse to get onto the bridge, cross it, then climb up the abrupt side of the crevasse.

Joe captured that moment. "That was an awesome experience to walk across that bridge and look down into the depths of the crevasse. I am guessing that you could see down about 50 feet to blue ice before it curved away to something deeper and more terrifying. As we were setting up the pickets for the belay, I was wondering if we had enough equipment to ratchet someone out of there. I hoped we did not have to try."

As frightening as the crevasse was, there was a sense of beauty about it, too. "It would have been nice to stand in the middle of the bridge for a couple of minutes to take a bunch of pictures, but it isn't nice to tease Mother Nature," Joe said.

With good anchors and roped belays, we protected each of our climbers across. Because the snow bridge was the only way to cross the deep crevasse and forced every climbing party to one point, the route above on the Ingraham Glacier was well-marked, stamped into the snow by hundreds of boots. We could use their steps as we moved up the steepest section to the crater rim. Seven hours of continuous climbing had brought us to the rim at about nine a.m. From there we climbed down into the crater and walked across it to reach the 14,410-foot summit called Columbia Crest, the highest part of the western rim of the crater, half an hour later. Walking inside the crater rim of a volcano is thought-provoking. I tried to imagine how high Mount Rainier would have been if it had not blasted off its top centuries ago.

It was windy and chilly at the summit, but we had climbed the whole route in only shirts, no jackets. The sky was partly cloudy. We had views of Mount Baker, Mount Adams, Mount Jefferson and Mount St. Helens. We could see Mount Hood and remember that only three days before, we had stood on that summit and looked at Mount Rainier in the distance. I could only contrast that sky and view with my first climb on the Mount Rainier and the serious blizzard we had faced. A mountain can have many personalities.

On the descent, we had to cross the snow bridge in the crevasse a second time. "I remember crossing the bridge on the way down and noticing that someone, either going up or down, had punched through the edge of the bridge. That made it even more fragile. I am guessing with the temperatures the way they were on that climb that the bridge did not survive another day. The ranger had made it clear to us that the crevasse was wide enough that going around it would be a very long route if it was even possible. I don't know what future climbers would have done."

We arrived back at Camp Muir at two thirty, cooked dinner, and went to bed at seven thirty. This time I had no trouble sleeping. On our second night in the stone hut, we had roommates. Two other groups of climbers joined us, and I heard them get up just after midnight to begin their ascents.

The morning of July 23 was clear and had unlimited visibility. We commented that it was the third anniversary of our climb to the summit of Mount Kilimanjaro. We packed up our food and equipment and left the hut at eight a.m. The snow was good going down, so we were able to boot ski and glissade, sliding both standing up and sitting down.

"Mount Rainier is more than a mountain. It is an experience," John said. "Whether you attempt to climb it or just gaze up at it from it's base, Mount Rainier is a peak that deserves reverence and respect. The sheer magnificence of the mountain cannot be overstated."

When we reached the parking lot, we looked back up to the summit of Mount Rainier. Having been up there, we could understand the size of the mountain better. John added, "The funny thing is that I felt more in awe of Rainier standing in the parking lot after the climb than when I was on the summit."

We felt good, having climbed Mount Hood and Mount Rainier in less than one week. Our 50 for Tibet project had completed one-fourth of the state highpoints in two months. There were complications ahead, however. We intended to climb Granite Peak in Montana and Gannett Peak in Wyoming, two of the most difficult of the state highpoints, in August. While we were in Oregon, John had talked with another company that was interested in buying his company. As soon as we got home, John became entangled in negotiations, and it was clear he could not leave while those were in progress.

We discussed this. The original plan was for John, accompanied by various friends, family members, and employees as they had time, to reach the highpoints of all fifty states in one year. If we postponed Granite Peak and Gannett Peak, it would be the following July or August before we could try them again. They are both major peaks deep in significant mountain ranges, meaning they have a limited window each year for safe climbing. If we postponed them, that would move them outside the original one-year goal.

By 2006, John had been co-owner or owner of ECHO Geophysical Corporation for twenty-five years. He had built a strong, reputable company, and if he had a chance to sell it, he needed to be in the office every day to deal with the flow of the discussions. Two months of traveling and climbing had also worn us down. We needed more time at home, and we needed to enjoy the climbs as we were doing them. It was time to restructure our guidelines.

We put Granite Peak and Gannett Peak on hold for a year. Interestingly enough, the prospective sale of ECHO Geophysical Corporation had caused us to pause and examine the 50 for Tibet project and where we were with it. We realized that the one-year goal was the least important part of the project. It sounded impressive at the beginning, but we now understood that what mattered was to continue the fundraising and awareness of the Tibetan situation indefinitely into the future.

The negotiations to sell ECHO Geophysical progressed slower than John had hoped. John remembered, "It was very difficult in July 2006 to focus on 50 for Tibet while being in negotiations with a company to potentially purchase my company in a multi-million-dollar deal. In fact, when we were taking a rest day in Seaside, Oregon, after climbing Mount Hood, I had a one-hour phone conversation with representatives from the other company trying to work on a timeline to get a deal done. In addition, I remember on the descent from the summit of Mount Rainier in Washington, as we approached Camp Muir, that my mind wandered towards the ongoing negotiations instead of focusing on the downclimb. So, it was a big part of my life in July and early August that was, at times, on the forefront of my mind."

Our trip to the Northwest had been excellent. Mount Hood and Mount Rainier are classic mountains by any standard, and we had succeeded on both. We had had good weather, and we were feeling stronger as we climbed peak after peak. We were working well as a team, planning our trips effectively, and moving efficiently on the mountains. Our list of accomplished peaks was growing, and we were feeling good about the 50 for Tibet project. We knew from the start that it was a great idea, but to see the pieces fitting into place was satisfying for all of us. These two peaks only added energy to our project.

When the Dalai Lama visited Denver in September 2006, Team HighPoint was invited to meet with him. Steve Gardiner shakes hands with the Dalai Lama at the Inverness Hotel in Englewood, Colorado.
Photo by Dennis McKinney.

Chapter 5

The Dalai Lama
September 17, 2006

With Granite Peak and Gannett Peak postponed, and John involved in negotiations for the possible sale of ECHO Geophysical, the pace of the 50 for Tibet project slowed down.

In researching the 50 for Tibet project, John noticed that one state highpoint was on private property. It is Charles Mound, 1,235 feet high, in Illinois. It is possible to climb higher in Illinois than Charles Mound by going to the top of the Willis Tower (formerly the Sears Tower, elevation 2,033 feet) in Chicago, but Charles Mound is the highest natural point of land. Charles Mound is only open to the public five weekends per year. Luckily, John caught this in time so that he and a couple of others could make a quick weekend trip in early August before it closed for the year. Planning for such contingencies makes a project as large as 50 for Tibet even more difficult.

We followed that trip with a three-day visit to Idaho to climb Borah Peak on August 7. As we drove toward Borah Peak, we could see the fault line of the Borah Peak earthquake, which happened in October 1983. The quake measured 7.3 on the Richter Scale, killed two people and caused $15 million in damage, and was felt throughout the northwestern United States and southern Canada. The epicenter was just west of Borah Peak, and the initial shock was followed by at least twenty aftershocks of 4.0 or greater over the next ten months. The road to Borah Peak crosses the fault line, a twenty-two-mile long surface ground rupture that resulted from a nine-foot vertical displacement in the area. The valley dropped eight feet and Borah Peak raised one foot during the spectacular event. We hoped our climb on Borah Peak would be a calmer day.

The trail through the trees on Borah Peak gains a vertical mile over four miles of distance and has earned the nickname "The Hill From Hell." As we left the trail through the trees at sunrise, a brief rainstorm gave us a rest break before we tackled "Chicken Out Ridge," an exposed rocky buttress with solid handholds and footholds. As its name suggests, it convinces many climbers to turn around. The scramble up the gray limestone ridge to the 12,662-foot summit gives excellent views of the glacial-carved valleys and endless peaks of the Lost River Range in the Challis National Forest. This ascent was Highpoint #15 for our group.

John kept busy with the details of trying to sell his company, but managed to get away for one more late-August trip to 13,528-foot Kings Peak in Utah. The group hiked in to a high camp at timberline and saw several moose along the trail. The next morning, David and John finished the climb to the summit, spending an hour on top admiring views of the Uinta Range. They took a shortcut trail down and were hit by thunderstorms and lightning for much of the descent.

By that time, I was coaching the cross country team at Billings Senior High School and preparing to return to school for the start of classes, so I missed the trip to Utah as well as the group's trip the first week in September to Pennsylvania to climb Mount Davis (3,213 feet) before continuing on to Backbone Mountain (3,360 feet) in Maryland, Spruce Knob (4,863 feet) in West Virginia, Ebright Azimuth (448 feet) in Delaware, and Kittantinny Mountain (1,803 feet) in New Jersey.

"On the day we planned to climb Mount Davis, the highpoint of Pennsylvania, Tropical Storm Ernesto was moving in," John said. "As we drove to the state park where Mount Davis is located, the squall lines of pelting rain and high winds ripped branches off

A Journey Supporting The Rowell Fund

the trees and onto the rain-soaked road, making the debris field in our car's headlights seem surreal. We arrived at Mount Davis in Pennsylvania late at night, and hoping to avoid the storm the next day, we decided to hike up it in the blackness of night. We reached the observation tower on top at midnight in the middle of the storm. It was a very different feeling there than on any other highpoint."

Remnants of that storm followed the team the next day on Backbone Mountain in Maryland. A solid, steady rain fell as they hiked through dense forest for two hours on a muddy trail. Even in Gore-Tex jackets, they were soaked by the time they reached the summit.

Another interesting moment happened when the group reached Ebright Azimuth in Delaware just in time to meet the owner of the property. "We thought it was significant that the highpoint in America's first state is owned by an English woman who had collected a lot of stories about the area and people who have visited the highpoint," John said. "When she bought the property twenty-eight years before our visit, she didn't know it included the state's highpoint. Nobody cared then, but she gets a lot of visitors now."

Admiring the spectacular view from the summit of Kings Peak in Utah, David Baker takes a few moments' rest. The easiest route requires a 28.8 mile round-trip hike.
Photo by John Jancik.

Throughout the planning for 50 for Tibet, awareness of the Tibetan plight had been one of the primary goals of the project. Helping people understand how the Tibetans were living under Chinese occupation was a constant topic of conversation.

John Ackerly, then-President of the International Campaign for Tibet in Washington, DC, and the climber who met me as we both walked onto the summit of Mount Whitney in California, said, "50 for Tibet has been a great boost in the efforts to find support for Tibetans who are struggling to preserve their country's environment and culture."

That was exactly what we wanted to accomplish, so it seemed more than timely that the Dalai Lama visited the United States, and one of his stops included Denver.

On Saturday, September 16, he would be part of an event called Peace Jam held at the University of Denver. The agenda featured short speeches by ten Nobel Peace Prize winners, including Archibishop Desmond Tutu, Costa Rican President Oscar Arias, the Dalai Lama, and others. Then, the Dalai Lama would speak on his own the next day at the Pepsi Center in downtown Denver. John was able to get tickets for both events.

My wife Peggy, daughter Denby, and I drove to Denver. We attended the Peace Jam event and enjoyed the speeches by the Nobel laureates. That evening, I got a call from John Jancik. John Ackerly had been able to arrange a brief private meeting between the climbers from the 50 for Tibet project and the Dalai Lama the next morning at the hotel where the Dalai Lama was staying. I asked what was appropriate dress to meet the Dalai Lama and John Ackerly said, "He doesn't care about clothing. He cares about your heart. Wear a nice smile."

John Jancik, members of his family, and I waited several long minutes in the Inverness Hotel lobby. I could not sit. I could not stand still. I have met national educational leaders, famous authors and presidents of the United States, but I can't remember ever being so excited to meet one person. I had read several of his books and seen him interviewed on TV. I knew his voice and his hearty laugh.

I couldn't wait to experience those firsthand.

Finally, an assistant to the Dalai Lama walked into the lobby and asked us to follow him. He led us upstairs and to a place where the hallway widened into a sitting room. He explained the Dalai Lama would pass down the hallway and through the sitting room on his way to his first meeting of the morning. He asked us to wait. We assured him we were not going anywhere.

A few minutes later, several monks walked down the hallway, and right behind them was the Dalai Lama. He greeted each of us and shook our hands. He thanked us for helping the people of Tibet through the fundraiser. He said he was happy to see that we cared about his people and that we were doing something meaningful to help them. He explained, "We are not seeking independence from China, but autonomy within China. It is an idea we call the Middle Way. We can find a balance that will help everybody."

It reminded me of a passage he had written in *My Tibet*, the book Galen Rowell had organized featuring Galen's photos and the Dalai Lama's words. He wrote, "When we look from a distance, the Tibetan situation doesn't seem nearly so hopeless. If we compare the strong force of China and the weak position of Tibet—only 6 million Tibetans and one thousand million Chinese—it's clear why the outside world wants to be good friends with China: for practical reasons, for reasons of power, but not for true friendship. Because of political sympathy for China, it has been very difficult for governments of major powers to support Tibet. This is reality, but beneath this reality the Tibetan issue lives on. Not only is it alive, but also it gains more and more strength. Time is an important factor. Back in the sixties and seventies much of the outside world believed the propaganda that the Chinese had done something good for Tibet by introducing the communist system. But the Chinese have proved equally expert at discrediting themselves. Our voice does not have to be so strong to overpower them, only strong enough to be heard after their latest version of events discredits a previous one."

I had a copy of *My Tibet* with me. I gave the Dalai Lama the book, and he signed it. Then John Jancik gave the Dalai Lama one of the 50 for Tibet flags we had been carrying with us. John explained that it had been to the highest point in twenty-one states. The Dalai Lama smiled and accepted the flag. We stood next to him for a photo, and then he moved on down the hall to his morning meeting.

We were stunned. No one spoke. We walked back down the stairs and out into the parking lot in front of the hotel. Someone said, "Can you believe what just happened?" After all I had read about him, it had been amazing to talk with him, to look him in the eye and listen to his ideas about his country and the world.

In the afternoon, we went to the Pepsi Center for the Dalai Lama's presentation. As we listened to the Tibetan flute music and watched the Tibetan dancers, I thought about the first time I saw how the Dalai Lama inspired the people of Tibet. It was 1988, and I was traveling across Tibet to the north face of Mount Everest with a group called the Wyoming Centennial Everest Expedition. Each time we stayed in a village or stopped along a roadside, the people would ask us, "Dalai Lama photo?" By that time, he had been gone from Tibet for almost three decades, but he was still their spiritual leader, and they wanted any connection to him they could get. Most of the people asking for the photos would not have been alive when he fled Tibet to live in exile in India.

In Lhasa, the capital of Tibet, our Everest team had time to wander the streets, talk with the Tibetan people, and get a sense of what was happening in the country. Every time I walked through the city, the most astounding thing to me was the laughter. The Tibetans laugh loud and hard, and as they walk down the street, often arm-in-arm, they sing. To me, they are the happiest people on earth, even though they have been an occupied nation since 1950.

The night before we left Lhasa for Mount Everest, a high lama stopped at the hotel to meet with us. He blessed our expedition, wishing that we would travel and climb safely and return everyone to Lhasa at the end of our climb. He talked about the beauty of the Everest region and then said he would like to talk with us, to answer any questions we might have.

Our group asked many questions about Buddhism, about the history of Tibet, about the changes that had taken place. One question has stayed with me for all the years since that night in Lhasa. One climber asked, "When we walk down the street, we see the Tibetan people laughing and singing. They live in one of the most oppressed countries in the world. How can they still be happy?"

"First, you must understand one thing," the lama responded. "We have a different view of life than you do in America. We see things from a longer point of view regarding time. We understand that at this time, China has taken control of our country. That is now. We believe that we will have Tibet back. It might be two thousand years, but we will someday walk in our own Tibet again. That is why we can still sing and be happy and smile. We know our Tibet will return to us in the future."

When I think of how impatient people often get, when they need to wait a few minutes in a line, or when they need to wait a few days for a project to get finished, I am amazed at the view the high lama expressed about the people of Tibet. I decided to carry that attitude, as best I could, with me to Mount Everest. I knew the difficulty of climbing Everest, the highpoint of the world, would be challenging throughout our expedition.

It was challenging. We climbed up the East Rongbuk valley and set up an advanced base camp at the bottom of the North Col. We climbed through the icy blocks of the North Col and set Camp IV on the top of the Col. From there we headed up the North Ridge, placing Camp V at 25,500 feet. Then winds in excess of one hundred miles per hour battered our camps, tearing tents off the mountain and making it unsafe for us to continue. We climbed strong for fifty-seven days, but in the end, the wind proved to be more than we could handle. As the high lama requested, we returned to Lhasa with all of our team members safe and healthy.

As a high school teacher, I had one goal when I returned to Lhasa. I wanted to visit a Tibetan school. I wanted to see what education was like in this isolated country. I got directions to a high school, and on our last day in Lhasa, I took a hotel shuttle to the Barkhor Market and walked to the school.

I walked inside the gate to find a school which looks like a small college campus with broad walkways and several white buildings. I went up to the first adult I saw and asked if I could meet the English teacher. Just by chance I had found the headmaster, and he took me to the English teacher's office but he was absent, so the headmaster went to get him.

Soon after, I met Li, the English teacher, and we talked for twenty minutes in his office. Li is Chinese and had studied four years at a Chinese teachers' college. He had been in Lhasa for four years and said he was happy working there, although the Chinese personnel we worked with on our expedition made it clear that they viewed traveling and living in Tibet as a hardship, perhaps even a punishment along the lines of a Siberian-type exile.

Li has two classes each day, six days per week. His classes have fifty and forty-six students who are the equivalent of high-school seniors in America. They are seventeen and eighteen years old, and most will go on to college. They sit in rows of ancient wooden desks which hold two students each, and sit on square wooden stools, and have books and notebooks with very brown paper in front of them.

The instruction is in Chinese, except for classes in Tibetan and English. The school requires six years of English of all students.

When I entered the classroom, Li said, "Comrades, we have a visitor in our class today." He introduced me, and the students started clapping. Li turned to me and said, "Go ahead." He hadn't told me he was going to do this, so I really didn't know where to start, but one girl stood up and asked several questions. I answered them, questions about my home, our expedition, our travels. Other students stood up, asked questions, and politely stood while I gave my answers.

I had brought along a photo album, and the students loved it. I walked up and down the rows and explained the photos. I was teaching at Jackson Hole High School in Wyoming then, so I showed them photos of the Tetons, the town of Jackson, the high school, our home and my wife and our daughters. They liked best the photos of the school and students and were especially interested in pictures of my family.

The common response to each photo was "Bootiful."

Li had described his students as "very attentive." But as I spoke to them, they joked, turned around, did all the same things I saw in students in my own school. Kids are kids.

The hour passed quickly, and as I was leaving, I gave Li a stack of Jackson Hole postcards that he could share with the students. Li walked me to the gate, and we said goodbye.

From the school I walked back to the Barkhor Market to experience it one last time. The smell of juniper incense burning, the chant of the monks, the shouts of the money changers, the press of ladies selling jewelry, the voices of "Chang-a-money," "You, how much?" and "Om mani padme hum." The whole feeling of the market is special, and I believe that a circuit of the Barkhor Market is one of the most interesting walks I have taken in any country.

Yet, in spite of my joy at walking in the Barkhor Market, a sadness filled my heart. Even in 1988, Li, a Chinese teacher, addressed his students as "comrades," the greeting of the Communist Party. The instructional language of the schools in Lhasa had already changed to Chinese with Tibetan as a second language, like English. As anyone who has traveled in foreign countries knows, when our home language is removed from our daily lives, everything changes. The destruction of the Tibetan culture by the Chinese, beginning with the language, and moving out to all ways of thinking and acting, was systematic and complete.

Now, twenty-five years after I visited that classroom, I think about those students. They may have children who are now students in Tibetan schools. A full generation later, the transformation of the language and thinking must be complete. How many ideas and customs that make up one of the most unique societies in the world, have been lost? Can they ever be replaced?

At the Pepsi Center in Denver, the Dalai Lama spoke for two hours. His smile and gentle laugh were infectious. He quickly had 20,000 people leaning forward, hoping to hear his wisdom. He talked of compassion for others, of avoiding the afflictive emotions and seeking a happy life, of doing what good we can in the time we have on this earth.

"Love and compassion are the center of all religions," he said.

"The main message of religion is to practice love and compassion." He added, "Compassion has a positive scientific effect in our brain."

The Dalai Lama said that the world's nations have become increasingly interdependent. "Force and violence are unrealistic today," he said. "We must solve our problems by peaceful means. Force creates more problems. War is the worst kind of violation. It is legalized violence, legalized murder."

Regarding the future of Tibet, "we are seeking genuine autonomy within China," the Dalai Lama said. He said the Chinese government often gives misinformation to its people. "China deliberately creates ignorance among its own people. This is wrong. A closed society is suicide."

One reason for the Dalai Lama's trip to the United States was to receive the Congressional Gold Medal from President George W. Bush. One month after we met him in Denver, the Dalai Lama was in Washington, DC, to receive the highest award the U.S. government can bestow on a civilian. The award drew strong protests from the Chinese government, but it was the third time that President Bush had met with the Dalai Lama in public.

John Ackerly sent John Jancik an invitation to attend the ceremony in the Capital Rotunda. John Jancik and his wife Terri Baker, along with several family members, attended. John said it "was an incredibly powerful and moving gathering. I was honored to witness the awarding of the gold medal to His Holiness the Dalai Lama."

The Dalai Lama, in a twenty-minute acceptance speech, thanked President Bush and the people of the United States for their continued friendship with the people of Tibet. He added, "This recognition will bring tremendous joy and encouragement to the Tibetan people, for whom I have a special responsibility. Their welfare is my constant motivation, and I always consider myself as their free spokesperson. I believe that this award also sends a powerful message to those many individuals who are dedicated to promoting peace, understanding and harmony."

Chapter 6

The First Year of 50 for Tibet
September 16, 2007

The Communist Party came into power in China in October 1949 and within months, the People's Liberation Army invaded Tibet, overcoming the limited Tibetan army. By October 1950, Tibetan troops surrendered and the Chinese authorities forced the Tibetans into signing a Seventeen Point Agreement which basically gave China full control over Tibet, although Tibet was assured some sense of autonomy.

Tibetans had little or nothing in common with the Chinese invaders, who repeatedly violated articles of the agreement. The two groups had separate languages and cultural backgrounds. The Tibetans were deeply united in their Buddhist religion and the Chinese Communists were anti-religion. It was a mix that simply could not happen.

Traditionally, many of the Tibetan people lived a nomadic existence. One of the changes brought about by the Chinese occupation was the transfer of thousands of Chinese citizens to locations within Tibet, taking over the lands used by the nomads and limiting the opportunities for growth by Tibetan business and agriculture.

In the years after the Chinese invasion, the destruction of Tibetan religious buildings and monuments was methodical. Over 6,000 monasteries were destroyed by People's Liberation Army troops.

Other religious and historic buildings were leveled. Protesters were detained, thrown in prison, or killed. More than 1.2 million people died, nearly one-fifth of Tibet's total population.

For decades, reports coming out of Tibet told of horrible conditions in the prisons, especially for the monks and nuns who chose to protest. Prisoners have often faced long periods in isolated cells, lack of food, lack of sleep, and other deprivations. Many have been tortured.

In the early years of Chinese occupation, few stories about these conditions reached the outside world. In more recent years, organizations like the International Campaign for Tibet have maintained lists of prisoners and their reasons for confinement, missing persons, and other human rights violations. ICT and other groups, including The Rowell Fund for Tibet, seek to share information about the situation in Tibet and how the people are affected by new developments and Chinese policies.

Because of the oppressive nature of the Chinese occupation, many Tibetans have chosen to flee the country, often following the Dalai Lama into India. They leave because they are not free to express themselves or to practice their religion or unique cultural traditions. Many Tibetan holidays are forbidden and many festivals can no longer take place. Chinese authorities control Tibetan schools, so many refugees are students who want to control their own educations, rather than submitting to the curriculum designed by the Chinese. Other Tibetans leave because they fear being arrested or persecuted for their political beliefs or actions.

As more and more Tibetans escaped, the Chinese cracked down on the routes used by the refugees. It has become harder for Tibetans to leave and more dangerous, as well. One highly publicized incident occurred in September 2006, when a 17-year-old Tibetan nun named Kelsang Namtso was walking with a group of refugees only minutes away from the Nepal border on Nangpa Pass (18,753 feet) when she was shot and killed by Chinese soldiers who initially claimed they had fired in self-defense. However, a Romanian mountain climber on Cho Oyu, a short distance away, had been filming the refugees and captured the shooting on video. He can be heard in the background saying, "They are shooting them like dogs." The video was broadcast by news stations throughout the world. Reports of other shootings of refugees have circulated through Tibet-support groups and news agencies.

One of the more disturbing developments in the Tibetan situation has been the practice of self-immolation, often by Tibetan monks. According to the International Campaign for Tibet, as many as one hundred and forty-six Tibetans have died by setting themselves on fire, with as many as eighty of those incidents occurring in 2012 alone. Because of the emotional nature of photos of a human being burning, these protests have had an impact on Tibetan supporters throughout the globe. The Chinese have struggled to suppress reports or photos of self-immolations, but cell phones and internet services have made it easier to get these gruesome images to the world outside Tibet.

The Dalai Lama has said he does not promote the self-immolations as a form of protest and fears that even such drastic actions will have little effect on changing Chinese policies and practices toward the Tibetan people.

He said, "The Chinese government wants me to say that for many centuries Tibet has been part of China. Even if I make that statement, many people would just laugh. And my statement will not change past history. History is history."

As often happens in the midst of tragedy, people who care are pulled together, united, and given a sense of direction. Such may be the case regarding the situation in Tibet. Famed travel writer Pico Ayer wrote, "One of the happier ironies of recent history is that even as Tibet is being wiped off the map in Tibet itself, here it is in California, in Switzerland, in Japan. All over the world, Tibetan Buddhism is now part of the neighborhood. In 1968, there were two Tibetan Buddhist centers in the West. By 2000, there were forty in New York alone."

Even though the Chinese authorities refer to Tibet as the Tibet Autonomous Region, it has been autonomous in name only. The Chinese claimed that their actions liberated Tibet from slavery and feudalism; however, as history since the Chinese invasion in 1950 clearly shows, the destruction of monasteries and other important buildings, the exile of the Dalai Lama, the fleeing of thousands of Tibetan refugees, the imprisonment and torture of protesters, the killing of more than a million citizens, and the continued oppression of Tibetan education, culture, religion and human rights, are designed to demonstrate Chinese control and are essentially an effective form of cultural genocide.

In early November, the 50 for Tibet group headed to the southeast. I was teaching, so I could not join them, but Joe Sears was able to join John, David, and others for a hike up Mount Rogers (5,729 feet) in Virginia. The team camped near the Mount Rogers trailhead and woke in the morning to find frost covering their sleeping bags, air temperature of fifteen degrees, and wind speeds of thirty-five miles per hour, giving them a "nippy start" to what was one of the coldest highpoints completed by the 50 for Tibet project. In the dark, Joe Sears was walking through the campsite and walked into a tree branch. "I could feel the branch go into my eye and move behind my eyeball. I checked it out and it seemed like I was OK, so I went on the hike, but I was worried that maybe I had done something to my vision. It was scary."

From Virginia, they moved on to Black Mountain (4,145 feet) in Kentucky; Mount Mitchell (6,684 feet) in North Carolina; Clingman's Dome (6,643 feet) in Tennessee; Sassafras Mountain (3,560 feet) in South Carolina; and Brasstown Bald (4,784 feet) in Georgia.

John called Sassafras Mountain "one of the unexpected pleasures of the highpointing journey. The beautiful autumn leaves were in full color and we had the highpoint all to ourselves. We had gorgeous views between the trees. We stayed for an hour enjoying the color, the forest, the quiet. Even the drive there, through the backroads lined with colorful forest, was remarkable."

On Mount Mitchell in North Carolina, the highest point east of the Mississippi River, a dozen members of the Himalayan Society joined John and the others for the hike. Mount Mitchell is in the Black Mountains which John called "one very pretty area, especially in the fall colors."

In December, it was time for some warm weather, so John scheduled the climb of Mauna Kea (13,796 feet) in Hawaii for the second weekend. Before the climb, however, we drove to the north coast of Oahu to spend an hour flying in a glider plane and another hour in a shark cage behind a boat near Haleiwa. The boat's crew threw chum into the water, and using diving masks and snorkels, we could see the sharks snap up the chum and circle endlessly around our cage. The captain said there were about twelve sharks, but they moved around us so frequently, that I would have had no idea how many were there.

The evening before we left for the Big Island and the climb on Mauna Kea, we went to Pearl Harbor and sat on the bay, watching the Arizona Memorial as the sun went down. From there, it was a short walk to Aloha Stadium, where we watched U2 perform the one hundred and thirty-first and final concert of their worldwide Vertigo Tour.

Early the next morning, we heard noise outside the hotel and looked out to see runners in the Honolulu Marathon passing on the street below us. We watched them, then went to the airport to fly to Kona on the Big Island. We drove partway up Mauna Kea—the highest mountain on earth if measured from the ocean floor—parked the SUV, and hiked the last 3,000 feet to the top, even though a paved road goes to within a short distance of the summit. The trail passed through terrain that looked like photos from the lunar surface. Not far below the summit, we found a small patch of snow on the north side of the mountain and threw snowballs in Hawaii.

In February 2007, the team was able to make two weekend trips. The first was to climb Guadalupe Peak (8,749 feet) in Texas, Black Mesa (4,973 feet) in Oklahoma, and Mount Sunflower (4,039 feet) in Kansas.

The team camped under the stars, and next day, on the trail to Guadalupe Peak, they saw a sunrise that was "second only to the one we saw from the upper slopes of Mount Rainier of all our highpointing adventures," John noted. "The wind on the summit was biting cold for Texas. We didn't expect it to be that cold, but from the summit, we could see forever."

The cold continued the next day on Black Mesa in Oklahoma. The team expected an easy walk to the top of the mesa, but found over two feet of snow at the base. John said, "The snow was crusty and we were postholing to our knees. It was exhausting work. We knew where the trail was, but there were no footprints in the snow, so we had to walk a mile and a half punching through the crust on the snow. It was better on the top of the mesa, because the large mesa was windblown and mostly bare ground. At the top, we had climbed above the fog, so we were looking out across the clouds."

Later that same day, the group visited Mount Sunflower, again walking half a mile through knee-deep snow, to reach the highpoint at dusk. "David almost broke a leg puncturing through the snow into a Kansas crevasse, a cattle guard," said John. Throughout the winter trip, the roads had been muddy and difficult to drive, making the weekend jaunt much more challenging than expected.

John Ackerly was able to join the group on the second February trip when we walked to Fort Reno in Washington, DC, which we termed an "extra credit" walk since it is not technically a state highpoint, before we went on to visit Campbell Hill near the flagpole in a school yard (1,550 feet) in Ohio and Hoosier Highpoint (1,257 feet) in the middle of a cornfield in Indiana.

In March 2007, no highpoints were reached, but in April, the team made one trip which included Britton Hill (345 feet) in Florida (the lowest state highpoint), Cheaha Mountain (2,407 feet) in Alabama, and Woodall Mountain (806 feet) in Mississippi.

"We had an absolutely beautiful sunset on Cheaha Mountain," John said. "We got some great photographs of the sunset, an orange ball peeking through the haze. We were surprised that the Talladega Mountains are more rugged and steep than you might think."

Alli Bannias from Parker, Colorado, administrative assistant at ECHO Geophysical, participated in the trip to Britton Hill in Florida. She said, "Northern Florida was very interesting. My favorite memory was being at a local restaurant, and suddenly, in the middle

A Journey Supporting The Rowell Fund

of our meal, someone brought out an American flag and everyone started singing 'God Bless America.' There was a lot of hooting and hollering from the other diners, and then everyone went back to their meal. The highest point of Florida itself was pretty. You simply got out of the car and stood on the highpoint. Pretty easy."

Two trips in May resulted in five highpoints including Eagle Mountain (2,301 feet) in Minnesota, Mount Arvon (1,979 feet) in Michigan, Timm's Hill (1,951 feet) in Wisconsin, Taum Sauk (1,722 feet) in Missouri, and Driskill Mountain (535 feet) in Louisiana.

Eagle Mountain in Minnesota is in the Boundary Waters Canoe Area, so I was excited to visit that peak. Just after college graduation in the 1970s, Joe Sears and I had worked for a summer at a wilderness camp at the end of the Gunflint Trail. It had been a summer of beauty and freedom, hiking and canoeing day after day, so I was eager to return to that scenic area. The hike on Eagle Mountain was on a glorious spring day, and we had the trail all to ourselves. The summit gave us a view into much of that splendid Boundary Waters landscape.

From Eagle Mountain in Minnesota, Bob Vite, Steve Gardiner, and David Baker take in the beauty of the Boundary Waters Canoe Area Wilderness and the Superior National Forest.
Photo by John Jancik.

Mount Arvon in Michigan presented a nice forest walk on a "new highpoint." Mount Curwood, a long forested ridge, had been the state highpoint until 1982 when a re-survey determined Mount Arvon was a foot higher. It can be a brutal business being a state highpoint.

John had grown up in Wisconsin so the hike on Timm's Hill was a homecoming to the "land of the Cheeseheads," as he said. He had hiked Timm's Hill before (in 1980 as his first state highpoint), but "it was a joy to do it as a part of the 50 For Tibet fundraising adventure, especially since fellow Wisconsin native and ECHO Geophysical colleague Bob Vite was able to join us for that highpoint."

On June 16, 2007, exactly one year after the first climb of the 50 for Tibet project on Mount Whitney in California, the group walked to Hawkeye Point (1,670 feet) in Iowa, near a silo at the end of a feed trough on a farm four miles south of the Minnesota border.

The original goal had been to complete all fifty state highpoints in one year. That goal proved to be unrealistic, yet the team did reach forty-two state highpoints, raised $87,000 in tax-deductible donations and pledges, and climbed over 62,000 feet of elevation gain in the first year of 50 for Tibet.

"I was very pleased with the progress that 50 for Tibet made in terms of highpoints reached and monies raised during its first year of existence," John said. "Unlike now where fundraising climbs and adventures are almost commonplace, back in 2006, it was a rarity. So, the success we achieved, especially considering we all had jobs and families, was something that made me proud."

The project involved many people as participants in the hikes and climbs. John Jancik had reached the top of all forty-two state highpoints during the first year. Terri and David Baker had been involved in many of the trips. Several ECHO employees, including Alli Bannias, Bob Vite, Cormac Dorsey, Jennifer Pauley, Jessica Morse, Marshall Kettner, and Heather Van Veldhuizen, had been on trips. Tony Rowell and John Ackerly had been able to go along on two highpoints each. Joe Sears and I had been on multiple hikes and climbs.

Dorsey, who lives in Lakewood, Colorado, appreciated being

invited along. "I think it is very generous of John to include employees as part of the 50 for Tibet project. It is such a great project, and even though it seems like the fate of Tibet is a done deal, and I don't see anything turning back as China becomes more powerful, perhaps more political pressure can help preserve some of the Tibetan culture."

Thinking about the first year, John Jancik said, "Every highpoint has been an adventure. We've met incredible people along the way, and even some of the states that we didn't expect to be very exciting have given us interesting stories or beautiful scenery. We've seen the East Coast from Maine to Georgia and a variety of landscapes from coast to coast."

John said a frequent question asked of the group is, "What is your favorite highpoint?"

"It depends on how you define favorite," he said. "I had always wanted to climb Katahdin in Maine and Hood in Oregon. Those were important to me. Then there was Mount Whitney, where our teams reached the summit at the same time from two sides of the mountain. We had a very emotional time remembering Galen and Barbara Rowell from the highpoint of their home state."

The first year of the project gave us many shared memories. "We've had a lot of fun together," John said. "It has been a challenge, and I know that I have come to several important realizations about myself and life. When 50 for Tibet started as a concept, an idea, to fund raise for The Rowell Fund, I was determined to help keep Galen and Barbara's legacy alive. However, during the course of 2006, the fundraising adventure became more and more a parallel passion to learn and assist Tibetans. To me, the journey had become much more than what I imagined when I first started thinking about doing state highpoints."

The challenges of the 50 for Tibet project were many. Travel logistics. Being away from home, work, and family. The hikes and climbs on the peaks. Despite the challenges, John never lost sight of the real reason behind the 50 for Tibet project.

"This is all being done for a humanistic cause," he said. "It's not just about the Tibetan people. It's about being fortunate to live in the

U.S. and recognizing that we have a moral obligation to our fellow human beings to preserve their cultures, whether it is the Tibetans or in other corners of the globe where peace and compassion have been replaced by violence and intolerance. When we met the Dalai Lama in September, he told us his wonderful culture is dying. That's a pretty powerful statement to hear from the lips of a nation's leader. I believe what we are doing is an important and universal cause."

The imposing north face of Granite Peak, Montana's highest mountain and the last state highpoint to be reached, highlighted in the early morning sun.
Photo by John Jancik.

Chapter 7

The Top of Montana
August 1, 2007

People who willingly face challenges in life often come up against one that becomes a nemesis. A baseball player who just can't get a hit off a certain pitcher. A hockey player who can't score against one rival team. A tennis player who can't win a specific tournament. Mountain climbers sometimes find that one mountain becomes that obstacle, and for John Jancik, the mountain that haunted him was Granite Peak, the highpoint of Montana.

He first tried to climb it in 1977 and turned around after he and his partner realized they were unprepared for the strenuous nature of the climb. He returned in 1979, better prepared, but limped off the mountain with a sprained ankle. He tried again in 1986, 1987, 1989, 2004, and the postponed trip in 2006. Equipment problems, snow conditions, bad weather, work obligations, and other problems seemed to plague him every time. During those years, he climbed more than one hundred other mountains, but Granite Peak always said no. We started joking with John that in the thirty years since he first attempted Granite Peak, the scoreboard read:

Granite Peak—7
John Jancik—0

We had kicked off the second year of 50 for Tibet in late June 2007 with nice hikes on Harney Peak (7,242 feet) in South Dakota and White Butte (3,506 feet) in North Dakota. John and Terri, along with family members, hiked the crowded trail up Harney Peak in South Dakota (later renamed Black Elk Peak). My wife Peggy and I, along with our daughters Romney and Denby, drove from our home in Montana, and met them two days later to hike up White Butte in North Dakota. It was a nice reunion to get so many friends together for a hike. Later that day, John and his group visited the marker for the Geographical Center of the United States in Butte County, South Dakota.

In July, the team returned to home turf by getting a group of eight up the southeast trail to the top of Mount Elbert (14,433 feet) in Colorado, the highest summit in the Rocky Mountains of North America. We had planned this climb for September 2006, but an early season snowstorm forced a postponement until 2007. Clear skies and calm air gave the group a beautiful day for climbing.

"It was an awesome accomplishment," said Alli Bannias. "There was no better feeling than reaching the top of Mount Elbert after hours of hiking and seeing out over the world. I haven't been able to replicate that specific feeling since."

As the administrative assistant at ECHO, Alli took on many extra duties while John and other employees were participating in the 50 for Tibet trips. "Working with 50 For Tibet was a unique opportunity that solidified a lot of my administrative and marketing skills," Alli said. "I had to be very persistent and tactful to contact local political representatives for letters of support, be on top of tracking donations, creating thank-you packets for donors, coordinating website updates, and even helping create marketing materials like t-shirts and brochures. Every skill that I learned during my time working for the 50 For Tibet non-profit organization I've been able to utilize in my career path going forward, and for that I'm very thankful for the opportunity."

The next day, we made a short drive into western Nebraska to Panorama Point, (5,424 feet) in the middle of a bison pasture. I had graduated high school and college in western Nebraska, but did not know anything about highpointing at that time. The visit to

A Journey Supporting The Rowell Fund

Panorama Point gave me a new view of my former home state. For John, it was also a family moment. "Having my daughter Sarah along on the Nebraska highpoint was a lot of fun. She got to see first hand all the aspects of what we do during highpointing such as the flag pictures and the signing of the summit register."

We tagged another extra credit project by visiting the nearby Tri-State Marker where the state boundaries of Nebraska, Wyoming, and Colorado meet. The main focus of the summer, however, would be getting John to the top of Granite Peak in Montana.

Alli Bannias (right) and John Jancik on the summit of Mount Elbert, Colorado's tallest mountain. This peak, at 14,433 feet, is the highest in the Rocky Mountains.
Photo courtesy of John Jancik.

John Jancik, David Baker, and I set out on July 31 into Montana's Absaroka-Beartooth Wilderness Area. As we began our trip, John said, "I was very pensive about going after Granite Peak for the eighth time. What would it take to break my string of failures? What was the climb like once we circled around to the top of the south face? What would the potentially volatile thunderstorm weather be like? Many questions rattled around in my brain as we packed up in Billings and climbed our way up to the Froze-To-Death Plateau. I knew that I was going after Granite Peak for quite possibly the last time in my life, so while I really wanted to reach the summit, I didn't want us to push so hard that we did something stupid. I wanted us to give the mountain our best effort, but also our smartest effort."

From our start above West Rosebud Lake, we hiked three miles and gained 1,200 feet to Mystic Lake. From the south side of Mystic Lake, we took the Phantom Creek Trail uphill through a series of twenty-six switchbacks as it climbs nearly 3,000 feet in just two miles. With backpacks loaded with three days of food, climbing ropes and equipment, tents, and other camping gear, we slowed our pace considerably. The afternoon sun beat down on us as we trudged up the steep trail. When we arrived at the top of the switchbacks, we left the trail and hiked across the expanse of the Froze-to-Death Plateau, admiring the alpine wildflowers in full bloom. At the southwestern end of the plateau, with the summit of Granite Peak in sight, we set up camp. Rocky Mountain goats played on the grassy slopes and sometimes circled near our camp, curious about the visitors in their neighborhood.

We had found a level camping spot, somewhat protected from the wind by a few large boulders. John and David set up a two-man tent, and I put up a much smaller one-man tent. The Froze-to-Death Plateau is notorious for wind and thunderstorms, and while we had crossed it during a sunny afternoon, the evening brought thick, dark clouds and a sense of coming storm. We ate dinner and talked about our plans for the morning.

The darkening sky brought rain that sent us inside our tents early. It was light for half an hour, but by dusk, the rain picked up, and during the night, pounded our tents. Lightning sparked the sky.

Thunder echoed off the mountains and through the valleys. We were dry inside, but with the rain, everything outside was soaked. I hoped the goats that had visited our camp were managing to stay safe. A flash of lightning and roar of thunder would wake me, but I would eventually drop off to sleep again. I just hoped it would clear in the morning and give us a fair shot at climbing the mountain. I really wanted to see John stand on the summit.

In the morning, the rain had stopped. John and I ate a quick breakfast and set out at five thirty across the last of the plateau toward Tempest Mountain. Just before Tempest, the route turns to the right and drops down into a saddle between Froze-to-Death Plateau and Granite Peak. It is discouraging to lose a few hundred feet of elevation the first thing in the morning, but it is the only way to reach the sharp ridge leading toward the Top of Montana.

When we reached the saddle, I looked up at the ridge. I had climbed it in 1981, so some of it looked familiar, but after twenty-six years, I hoped I could keep us on the right track.

I have read descriptions of this ridge that called it a razor blade or a meat cleaver. It is sharp and lets climbers know from the start that they are on a major mountain peak. The steepness of the Phantom Creek Trail, the size of the Froze-to-Death Plateau, the sharpness of this ridge, the technical climbing in the final 500 feet to the summit, and the notoriously bad weather mean Granite Peak has a very high failure-to-summit rate. Too many climbers underestimate these factors as they dream of reaching the remote summit.

One summer I worked at a local mountaineering store. It was a Sunday afternoon, and a woman came in and asked me about climbing Granite Peak. She had been to church that morning and said she was inspired to climb Granite Peak and pray for the people of Montana from the summit. I asked her if she had any previous mountain climbing experience. She didn't. She had no knowledge, no skills, no background, no equipment, but she wasn't discouraged. She needed to go to the top and pray. She was determined. I tried to be kind as I explained the difficulties and dangers. She asked me if I would take her up there. I said I would not until she had had more experience from climbing other mountains and had learned how to deal with the problems Granite Peak would deliver. She said she did not have time for that. She needed to go right away.

"Please be careful," I pleaded. "Granite Peak is not a beginner's mountain. It is serious and can be a very dangerous place. Yes, it is beautiful and would be an inspirational place to pray, but don't go there until you know what you are doing. I don't want to read about you in the newspaper."

She left the store, and I never heard anything more about her.

From our research on the fifty state highpoints, we knew that Granite Peak is rated the second hardest after Denali (Mount McKinley) in Alaska. We also knew that it was the last of the fifty state highpoints to be climbed. Denali had first been climbed in 1913, but it wasn't until August 23, 1923, that Granite Peak was summited. Many parties of climbers had been turned back on all sides of the mountain before Elers Koch led a team of Forest Service rangers to the top.

The knife-edge ridge rose high above us. We selected a route just to the left, or south, edge of the ridge and followed it upward. The rock was still wet from all the rain during the night, so we moved carefully. After an hour on that imposing ridge, we reached a narrow notch which drops off a thousand feet on each side. This spot has been the turn around point for hundreds of Granite Peak climbers.

When I had reached this notch in 1981, we needed crampons, ice axes, and a rope to cross it. It is only twenty-five to thirty feet across, but the exposure is extreme and a slip would be fatal. In 2007, the notch was dry. We walked across on loose stones and soon were scrambling up the summit block.

The nature of the climbing changed immediately. We had been on the sharp ridge, but now the rock was blocky and required hands as well as feet to move upward. I angled to the right, but quickly realized that I had taken a wrong turn. Above me were sections that were completely vertical. I didn't remember any climbing that severe from my earlier ascent, so I came back down and tried a section of rock closer to the south side. That was the right route. We scrambled up that section and rested on a flat area above it. From there, we could see the remainder of the climbing route. It was much steeper and more exposed than what we had been climbing, so John said he would like to tie on to the rope.

We have long had a rule that when one person in the group wants to have a rope, we stop immediately and put it on. No questions asked. The only guideline about that is that no one waits too long to ask for the rope. As soon as there is concern, we want anyone to feel comfortable to speak up. It is a rule that has served us well. We put on our seat harnesses and tied ourselves to opposite ends of the rope.

The rope was fifty meters or approximately one hundred and sixty-five feet long. I would climb out the full length of the rope, find a place to set up an anchor using the natural rock or pieces of protection I carried with me. When I had the anchor in place, I would yell for John to climb up, and I could protect him by pulling up the rope in a system called belaying. It is a system that has been used many years in mountain climbing and increases the safety tremendously. It does slow down progress, so we have to weigh the benefits of safety on one section with the idea that slowing down might put us in bad weather or some other hazard later in the day. From where we were when we put on the rope, I estimated that we had four hundred vertical feet to go to reach the summit. That would be three rope lengths or pitches.

With the rope attached to my seat harness, I climbed up a section of rock that forced the back of my helmet onto my backpack as I looked up. Fortunately, it had plenty of large handholds and footholds. It was exciting climbing, especially knowing that we were so close to getting John to the top of Granite Peak, a goal he had been working on for thirty years. When I climbed out a full rope length, I stopped, placed one piece of protection in a crack and tied a rope sling around a rock and attached the rope to that anchor. It was safe, so I called for John to climb up behind me. I pulled in the rope and secured him each time he moved upward.

When John reached me, I attached his seat harness to the anchor with a carabiner and removed my own attachment from the anchor. The next section of rock required me to climb straight upward,

80   Highpointing for Tibet

moving slightly to the right around a large, overhanging bulge of rock. Past that obstacle, I found a large ledge angling upward and to the left toward the summit. I moved onto the ledge and easily climbed up another full rope length. I repeated the process of setting up an anchor and belaying John up to me.

The final five hundred feet to the summit of Granite Peak in Montana are technically challenging and exposed. Steve Gardiner climbs around a rocky ridge onto the south face of the 12,807-foot mountain.
Photo by John Jancik.

When he was standing next to me, I attached his sling to the anchor, removed mine, and began what I thought would be the final pitch to the summit. I pointed upward and said, "We're almost there. We are going to make it." John looked up, but did not respond. I knew it had to be an emotional time for him, and I was glad I would be there to share it.

The ledge continued up a few more feet, then I climbed up steeper blocks of rock with good holds. After fifty feet of climbing on these blocks, I reached up for a handhold and pulled myself up. We were at the top. I stepped up and could see the flat, table-top rock that is the distinctive summit of Granite Peak. It was a fifty-foot walk away.

I quickly set up a final anchor and belayed John to the top. I expected him to yell or cheer when he reached me, but he was quiet. I respected that.

He later said, "When we reached the summit of Granite Peak, my emotions were almost numb. In some ways, I could not believe I had actually finally reached the roof of Montana. It had been thirty years of wondering what it would be like to stand on this peak's summit and now, I was finally there. I did reflect on the fact that I was very fortunate to have a climbing partner that was also a great friend and understood my strengths and weaknesses on a mountain like Granite Peak. Reflecting back, the time on the top seemed all too brief to me. It had taken me so long and so many times to get there, with the good weather we had at the time, I wanted to stay on the summit for an hour."

I gave John a hug and said, "I hoped that one day I would see you standing here on the summit of Granite Peak. That day is today. Congratulations."

We pulled out the flags and took a series of summit photos. We signed the copy of Galen's book and then we just stood there, looking. Granite Peak is dominant, the patriarch of Montana. We could see for miles in all directions. The thunderstorm during the night had been a concern, but on the summit, we had clear skies and comfortable temperatures. It was a Big Sky day.

We had left the final anchor in place, so when we left the summit stone, we went back to the anchor. I tied the rope to it and tossed it over the edge. John rappelled down the rope to the angling ledge and used the rappel rope to protect him as he walked down to the spot of the previous anchor. He waited there while I pulled out the summit anchor and then climbed down to him. I set up another anchor, tied the rope to it, and threw it over the edge again. The rope sailed out into the air and fell toward a large flat area below. Because of the steepness of the rock, we could not see the rope land, but I heard the rope hit and then heard a snort and scrambling sound. When I had tossed the rope over the edge, it had fallen down and landed on a mountain goat on the flat area. We watched him scurry across the next ridge and out of sight.

Two more short rappels helped us descend the steepest and most difficult parts of the climbing. We recrossed the narrow notch and then carefully worked our way down the sharp ridge. When we returned to the saddle between Granite Peak and Froze-to-Death Plateau, we paused for a drink of water. It was nice to know we had the serious part of the climb successfully behind us.

John and I returned to camp. David had been reading most of the day, so we told him about our climb, and he told us about the mountain goats that wandered through our camp. It was a happy group that night as we enjoyed the feeling of success on our team's forty-seventh state highpoint.

In the morning, we set out to cross the Froze-to-Death Plateau back to the Phantom Creek Trail. On the way, John and I decided to hike to the top of Froze-to-Death Mountain, a short climb since we were already on Froze-to-Death Plateau. From the summit, we looked back toward Granite Peak and had a good view of where we had gone the previous day. It was a view that for John, had been thirty years in the making. The scoreboard now reads:

Granite Peak—7
John Jancik—1

I think he considers the score even.

Chapter 8

Nearest the Sun
July 7, 2008

When the 50 for Tibet project began in June 2006, we had several goals—to increase awareness of the situation in Tibet, to raise money to support fellowships through The Rowell Fund for Tibet, and to provide team members with the challenging adventure of reaching the highpoint in each of the fifty states.

Two years later, the 50 for Tibet project had been successful beyond any of our expectations.

Through newspaper articles, television interviews and face-to-face contact with people across the nation, we helped many people understand the nature of the human-rights violations that had taken place in Tibet during half a century of Chinese occupation. Those same concerns became big news in the spring of 2008 when protests began in Lhasa on March 10 and spread across Tibet, with at least one hundred and twenty-five demonstrations taking place. The Chinese authorities arrested thousands of demonstrators, used violence on protesters, and killed Tibetans in at least eleven of the demonstrations. Protesters asked China to halt its human-rights violations and to begin a peaceful dialogue with the Dalai Lama. The Chinese responded with brutality.

In honor of the 2008 Summer Olympics in Beijing, the Chinese government launched a torch relay that would extend for 85,000 miles through twenty-one nations and six continents, the longest torch relay in the history of the Olympics. The torch, lit in a ceremony in Olympia, Greece, on March 28, was then taken to Athens where a small group of protesters complained about human-rights violations in China. From Athens, the torch went to Beijing for a tour of China, then on to a tour of several other countries.

In early April, the torch was scheduled for parades through London, Paris, and San Francisco. In each of those locations, growing crowds of protesters blocked the parade routes, attempted to douse the torch flame, and shouted "Stop Killing," "Shame on China," and "No Human Rights, No Olympics." Their actions were in response to the Chinese crackdown on Tibetan protesters in early March and China's long history of human rights violations against Tibetans and Chinese citizens alike.

To protect the Olympic torch on its tour, the Chinese sent along a team of guards whose tactics were often termed "heavy-handed" and whose members were referred to as "thugs." The torch parades continued, but were often shortened or rerouted to protect the torch and to thwart protesters. China called the protests "despicable" and claimed that the Olympic torch demonstrations created greater unity among the Chinese people and their goal of sponsoring the Olympic Games.

In their bid, China had promised freedom to international reporters, but as the games approached, reporters were forbidden to cover any negative subjects, and then, eventually many were expelled from the country. China initially agreed to issue protest permits and designate protest zones, but no permits were ever approved.

During the crackdown, many Tibetans were detained and tortured. Cell phones were confiscated and internet connections were blocked to create an information blackout. Several reports stated that Chinese police and informants were dressed in street clothes and were wandering through the cities to gather information and report on any dissent. One Tibetan, in exile, told the International Campaign for Tibet, "Roundups of Tibetans happen at night, usually around two o'clock in the morning. Every one is so petrified, whether they took part in any of the protests in March or not. When house-to-house searches began (after March 14), Tibetans had such a hard time hiding their secret pictures of His Holiness the Dalai Lama. There are grim tales of the dead and arrests. Family members of those missing went from prison to prison searching for their loved ones. Many are still missing."

Concern for the safety of Tibetans who spoke against the oppression in their country created worldwide interest in Tibet. Articles appeared in major newspapers everywhere and made the covers of *Time, Newsweek*, and other media giants. Links to hundreds of articles about Tibet raced through cyberspace.

Donations from many sources helped 50 for Tibet give strong support to The Rowell Fund for Tibet. By 2008, we had raised over $150,000. This money helped provide fellowships to Tibetan writers, musicians, and artists as they worked to preserve Tibetan culture.

By 2008, we had attempted forty-seven state highpoints and been successful on all of them. John had reached the summit of all forty-seven and other family members, friends, and employees had reached varying numbers of highpoints with him.

The theme of "Celebrating One Mountain Culture to Preserve Another" had stayed with us throughout our highpointing adventures. Celebrating the highpoints of the United States had been an interesting and educational journey for all of us.

The variety of the landscapes we had seen was an important part of the project. We had been on very easy highpoints like Britton Hill in Florida, Jerimoth Hill in Rhode Island, or Ebright Azimuth in Delaware. We had gone on gentle hikes like Mauna Kea in Hawaii, Harney Peak in South Dakota, Mount Mansfield in Vermont and Humphreys Peak in Arizona. We had seen breathtaking views of the Boundary Waters Canoe Area from Eagle Mountain in Minnesota, the lakes and thick woods surrounding Mount Katahdin in Maine, and the mountains of Idaho from Borah Peak. We had also made serious climbs on the twenty-two-mile route on Mount Whitney, the Mazama Route on Mount Hood in Oregon, the Disappointment Cleaver Route up and through the volcanic caldera on Mount Rainier in Washington, and the multi-pitch technical route above the Froze-to-Death Plateau on Granite Peak in Montana.

With Granite Peak finished, we had three state highpoints remaining. One was easy. It was Magazine Mountain in Arkansas. It had been passed by in a quirk in travel plans on an earlier trip from Missouri to Louisiana. A quick weekend trip let us hike up that peak and spend several concerned moments back at the car removing the many ticks we picked up on the walk.

That left two difficult highpoints. Gannett Peak in Wyoming is a six-day climb involving a long approach hike carrying all the climbing gear needed to ascend a glaciated peak in the Wind River Mountains. Denali in Alaska requires more than three weeks of serious mountaineering on an extremely cold, windy mountain.

We scheduled Gannett Peak for late summer 2008 and Denali for June 2009.

Again, work conflicts and family concerns made us postpone Gannett Peak in 2008. In the spring of 2009, we didn't seem to have the drive necessary to take on Denali. Perhaps it was the amount of climbing and traveling we had done over the previous three years. Perhaps we had focused so much energy for the last three years on 50 for Tibet that we needed a break and a chance to climb something not directly related to the project. Perhaps it was because John, Joe, and I were by then, in our mid-fifties and were losing interest in extreme mountaineering projects. We had certainly had our fair share of exciting climbs over the years, but did we really want to push as hard as Gannett Peak and Denali would require? These were questions that we started asking ourselves.

With those questions came other ideas. John and Joe had often expressed the desire to climb over 20,000 feet of elevation. I had done that on Everest in Tibet, on Huayna Potosi in Bolivia, and on Aconcagua in Argentina. I wanted to see if we could take them to that elevation. Yes, Denali would have been above that elevation, but the questions we had about going on a month-long expedition lingered. We came up with another possibility—Chimborazo in Ecuador, 20,564 feet high. As the highest peak in the country, we could easily call it the Top of Ecuador Expedition and continue our pattern. The biggest difference would be that instead of needing a month to climb, Chimborazo requires two days. Could we take the 50 for Tibet concept and expand it to international summits, as well?

I had first seen Chimborazo twenty-six years earlier. It was January 1983. My wife Peggy and I had just finished a year of teaching at the American School of Lima, Peru, and we were on a three-month journey around South America. Our first stop outside Peru had been Ecuador, and we had quickly fallen in love with the country. I knew someday I wanted to return to climb Chimborazo.

I found myself thinking about 20,564-foot peak many times as Peggy and I ventured through Bolivia, Chile, and Argentina. By the time we got to Uruguay in late February, I wrote a letter to Joe Sears, telling him about Ecuador and my dream of returning there to climb.

We talked about Ecuador from time to time, but years passed, and we were involved in many other climbs. Then, in 2009, the goal of reaching 20,000 feet came up again. The idea of glaciers on volcanoes on the equator was intriguing. In addition, the summit of Chimborazo, because of the equatorial bulge, has the distinction of being the point farthest from the center of the earth. If that point was farthest from the center of the earth, it was also the point on Earth nearest the sun.

Thus, we more often referred to the Top of Ecuador Expedition as the Nearest the Sun Expedition.

We wanted to get in at least one good training climb before we went to Ecuador, so we settled on Mount Shasta (14,162 feet) in California. We had all seen photos of the beautiful peak, and we knew it was a long, hard day to reach the summit. It would be a challenging climb and would get us over 14,000 feet, a good head start toward our goal of reaching 20,000 feet in July. I was also interested in Mount Shasta because it is in northern California, not far from Ashland, Oregon, where my oldest daughter, Greta, had gone to college and was still living. She would be able to join us on the trip.

I flew into Medford, Oregon, rented a car, and picked up Greta in Ashland. We drove to the town of Mount Shasta and met Joe Sears and John Jancik, ate dinner, and went to the campsite. We camped out without tents and paid the price for it during a rainstorm in the middle of the night. We ended up sleeping in our cars.

We were up in the dark on June 13 and hiked through the forest to the Sierra Club's Horse Camp at 7,884 feet. We took a short break there, then climbed up the snowfield to Lake Helen at 10,400 feet. It is a common camping spot even though the lake is usually frozen and covered with deep snow. We stopped to eat and drink. After the break, Greta left to hike back to the cars. Joe, John, Jen Pauley, and I set out toward the summit. The four of us were scheduled on the Nearest the Sun Expedition, so it would be a good chance to see how we were all doing in terms of fitness and acclimatization.

We used crampons and ice axes to ascend through the rocky section called the Red Banks. Above, the route moved on to a snowy ridge with the final summit block above that. We could see the route well in spite of the thick clouds all around us.

That long final ridge seemed endless. I felt more tired than I expected. It was hard to keep a rhythm. I usually feel very good at 13,000 and 14,000 feet, but that day on Mount Shasta, I was not doing as well as I had hoped. I stayed with my teammates, but struggled the last hour to the summit.

On top we took our photos with the flag, but it was quick. It was cold and windy, so we only stayed a few minutes before setting out to climb down the snowy ridge. While we were descending the ridge, the clouds came down on us. Our visibility dropped, and I was concerned about finding the right notch to go down through the Red Banks. At the base of the snowy ridge, snow fell. We stopped to put on rain jackets and mittens. In the time it took to put on the jackets, the snow turned to rain, then heavy rain. We climbed down through the notch in the Red Banks and just below there, we could see the snow slope beneath us was in excellent shape, so we sat down and slid on the seat of our pants, a glissade protected by having our ice axes at our sides. We were able to slide several hundred feet to just above Lake Helen.

The rain increased, and by the time we arrived at Lake Helen, it was a heavy downpour. It rained hard until we were well below

Horse Camp and hiking in the trees. I could really feel the tiredness caused by more than fourteen hours of hiking and gaining and losing over 7,000 feet. The heavy rain only made that time and distance more exhausting.

Joe's sister Margaret and her husband Rick had driven with Joe from Kennewick, Washington, to see Mount Shasta and spend some time walking in the area. When we arrived back at the campground, tired and wet, Margaret and Rick led us to the back of the campsite where we found a picnic table covered in a checkered table cloth topped with cheese and crackers, wine, and juice. All climbs should end in such style.

We traveled to Ecuador on July 1 and spent two days walking around the capital city of Quito. At 9,000 feet, it was good training for us as we prepared for Chimborazo. We decided to go on a training climb on a peak called Iliniza Norte. It is 16,817 feet high and would give us a good indication of how ready we were to attempt 20,000 feet. We hired a Jeep and driver to transport us to the trailhead. Again, we were in heavy fog as we climbed up the route, but we climbed easily and quickly through the paramo, a landscape of low shrubs, and onto a rocky ridge featuring stone towers glazed with rime ice. It was truly one of the most beautiful sections I have seen on a mountain, and we were in awe as we climbed through it. We had no view of the surrounding countryside, but the mountain right in front of us was glistening.

John remembered that "the rime ice we encountered on the mountain was as beautiful as it was intimidating to climb through. I will never forget watching Steve lead us through sections of that ice in fog and mist."

After climbing through the icy towers and up the rough ridge, we spent ten minutes on the breezy, freezing summit before making a hasty descent. We had climbed Iliniza Norte but had never seen it. The next day, we finally saw the route we climbed on a poster in a travel agency in downtown Quito. Climbing to just below 17,000 feet gave us confidence that we were ready to attempt Chimborazo and our goal of getting Joe and John to 20,000 feet.

Iliniza had been a good climb, but Chimborazo was the centerpiece of the expedition. It is a massive block of a mountain and in the light of a midnight full moon, the icy ridges of Chimborazo were gleaming white, stretching thousands of feet into the sky above us. The air was chilly, perfect for the effort climbing would require. A thin layer of clouds filtered the moonlight, but it was still bright enough to climb without headlamps, just as we had on Kilimanjaro.

At midnight, we left the Whymper Hut at 15,500 feet. The summit was more than 5,000 feet above us, and we hoped to stand there by eight in the morning. We expected a long, strenuous night.

The first hour of climbing was on a marginal trail over crumbled lava. We crossed a flat basin, climbed onto a ridge, and followed it directly toward the first glacier. At the ice, we stopped to put crampons on our boots. The temperature had dropped considerably since we had left the hut, and our fingers were numb working with the straps to secure the crampons. The wind was increasing, and we were happy to start climbing again.

We climbed a switchback section called the ZigZag to reach the bottom of a long ramp known as The Corridor. This ramp turned us to the right, and we passed below some steep, ice-crusted cliffs below a large rock tower called The Castle. We knew that when we reached The Castle, we would turn onto the main ridge and be on a direct line toward the summit. We were excited about that, but more concerned that the wind speed was increasing rapidly and the temperature continued to fall.

We climbed across The Corridor, and near the upper end, we faced a wind that was staggering. Sleet cut into our faces as we confronted a new hazard—the wind was collecting small rocks from the cliffs above and throwing them down on us. We had rocks bounce off our helmets and backpacks. One larger rock crashed into my shoulder. I heard rocks banging against the boulders around me. It was as if we had somehow walked into a geological shooting gallery.

"The storm on Chimborazo was my first experience with such high winds on a climb" Joe said. "It seemed even more intense because it was at night. It was an uneasy feeling to be walking up the mountain with the wind whipping us around, debris ricocheting

A Journey Supporting The Rowell Fund

off our bodies, and those pings in our ears of ice, pebbles, and small rocks striking our helmets."

The wind made Joe focus on the ground "five feet in front of me. We didn't dare look up for fear of being hit in the face with ice fragments or rocks. It was an interesting transition. It seemed as though one minute it was a nice quiet evening with excellent climbing conditions, and then we just walked into gale force winds. I was thinking that if we kept on climbing that we might run out of

Rime ice creates a fairyland effect as Steve Gardiner searches for a route through the rocky pillars at 16,500 feet elevation on Iliniza Norte in Ecuador.
Photo by John Jancik.

the wind."

However, the storm increased. We sat down on the glacier. Because of the wind, we were shouting at each other, even though we were only a foot or two apart. We had no reasonable choice but to abandon the climb.

"It was the right decision to turn around when we did," Joe said. "It was an awesome view the next morning of the clouds whipping around the top of the mountain. It had to be at least 100 mile per hour breezes up there. If only we had been there a day earlier when the conditions were perfect."

"The attempt on Chimborazo was very disappointing," John said. "The day we arrived at the Whymper hut, the skies were partly cloudy to mostly clear and winds were reasonable. However, after we started our summit attempt early the next morning, everything seemed to fall apart. First, the wind was howling off the mountain at speeds well in excess of fifty mph. Rocks, pebbles, and sand, seemingly everything, were being picked up and pelting us to the point where we could not even face into the wind. Second, I was having major difficulty with my crampons staying on. I had used the exact same set on Mount Shasta a month earlier, and they performed excellently. Frustration was mounting. Last, after the first two issues began to dominate the ascent, I came down with a moderate headache. While not debilitating, it was enough to convince me that, with the high wind and crampon problems as well, it was not my day to reach the summit. As it turned out, it was no one's day to reach the summit."

We could see one other climbing team above us, and four others were following. No one had much hope with the weather conditions deteriorating so quickly. We were at 17,500 feet. A lot of mountain remained, and we could hear the roar of the wind racing across the summit. It was getting dangerous, and it was worse above us.

All six teams turned back that night. We didn't stand on the summit of Chimborazo, the point on Earth nearest the sun. We did, however, experience an impressive storm on a great mountain, dealt with it appropriately, and spent time in Ecuador with friends. Not a bad way to spend part of a summer.

Chapter 9

The Top of the British Isles
July 1, 2010

Five adventures on five highpoints in five countries. That's what we were after when John and I set out for the Top of the British Isles trip.

Our trip to Ecuador and Chimborazo in 2009 had given us motivation to try other international highpoints and expand our 50 for Tibet project. When John called and asked if I was interested in climbing in the British Isles, I immediately agreed. I had seen this area in 1974, when, as a junior in college, I had arranged an exchange program to study English literature at the University of London. I visited the Lake District to see the homeland of the poets Keats, Shelley, and Wordsworth, but at that time, I hadn't climbed any mountains, so I never dreamed that three decades later I would get the chance to go back and climb some of the beautiful mountains I saw in the Lake District and North Wales.

The Top of the British Isles adventure started in the parking lot of the rental car company. I volunteered to drive first, and as soon as I put the car in gear, I saw another car coming directly toward me. I instinctively swerved to the right and he swerved to his left. I turned more to my right and he turned more to his left. Then I realized I was wrong. Pass on the left. I turned left, we passed each other, and we were officially driving in Great Britain.

We had landed in Glasgow, Scotland, and drove north to Fort

Williams. We decided to take an afternoon walk near the base of Ben Nevis, at 4,406 feet the highpoint of Scotland. Fittingly, a bagppiper was standing at the trailhead playing traditional Scottish music.

Our overall plan was to climb one day, drive the next, alternating as we moved to and up the five British peaks.

We returned the next morning to climb Ben Nevis. We had heard about the heavy fog in the British Isles, and though we could see fine at the trailhead, thicker clouds hovered above us. We had expected this type of weather, but our anticipation did not prepare us for how thick and blinding the fog could be. The first two hours were mostly clear, but after that, we climbed into the heavy clouds. The rocky summit block is a mass of boulders, a nightmare for any climber in fog because all the features appear the same. There is no distinction or sense of direction. Previous climbers had constructed large rock cairns the size of a man strategically placed along the pathway. Two very dangerous cliff faces are near the summit, and straying from the route could be a serious error. We picked our way carefully, but the fog was so thick that, at times, we could not find one cairn before leaving the last one.

Near the summit, we met a couple from Florida who had turned back, concerned about the lack of visibility and the 2,000-foot cliff on the northeast face. With such poor visibility, the cliff was a concern for any climber. We passed the place where they had turned back, and in five more minutes, we stumbled upon the triangulation point that marks the official summit. The couple had been so close, but with the visibility at fifty feet, they had no idea where the highpoint was.

Even though it was late June, we were wrapped in Gore-Tex jackets against the damp cold and steady drizzle. The dense fog had limited our views and photo opportunities, but we were very excited to have our first British Isles highpoint completed. We hiked back to the valley and drove south into Carlisle, England, for the evening.

Near Carlisle are the remains of Hadrian's Wall, a fifteen-foot-high barrier built by the Romans about 122 AD to protect the northern frontier of the Roman Empire. In ancient Roman times, the seventy-three-mile long wall had thirty forts, and many sections of the wall and fort ruins are still visible today. We visited the fort at Birdoswald before driving on to the Lake District in northern England, where we camped near Wastwater Lake at Wasdale Head.

As we hiked up Scafell Pike (3,210 feet), the tallest peak in England, on the morning of June 25, we had good views toward the summit, but as we approached, the clouds moved in and again blocked our visibility at the top. We were on the summit alone, until an English hiker walked up a couple of minutes later. He told us an interesting story about taking sixteen months off work to be part of a crew involved in an around-the-world yacht race. He had visited ports everywhere and told us about his life aboard the boat. They had been successful during the race and led the field for the final several legs before coming up two points short on the last day of the competition. We spent a few more minutes on the summit, unfurled the American flag on England's highpoint, and then hiked back down into the valley.

Northern Wales is a land of forested mountains, whitewater rivers, and cobblestone villages. On an earlier visit, I had hiked up to the lake Llyn Llydaw near the village of Llanberis and seen Mount Snowdon. I had a strong vision in my head of that lake and the view up to the snowcapped peak. Unfortunately, on this trip, I did not get a repeat of that spectacular view. Clouds had become our constant companions by now, so we were not surprised that the entire ascent of Snowdon was foggy. As we neared the summit, we could hear the engine of the train that brings tourists up the other side of Mount Snowdon. We could not see the train, but could hear the wheels clicking on the track. The tourists had picked a bad day to take a sightseeing train. There would be no views.

At the summit, we joined the tourists inside the mountaintop cafe for a cup of hot tea before hiking back down. On the descent from Snowdon, John stepped aside on the trail to allow a group of about fifteen hikers to move upward. He made a comment about how the group members seemed to be smiling and happy. One man paused near John and said, "Actually, it's a grimace." A few seconds later, his teammate added, "I might be smiling, but it's only because I'm in denial."

To set up the fourth peak, we flew across the Irish Sea to Dublin and drove across Ireland in the afternoon to reach Killarney in County Kerry, the town nearest the Irish highpoint of Carrauntoohil (CARE-un-tool). Traditional Irish music spilling out of the pubs into the streets of Killarney set the mood for our fourth highpoint on June 27.

We were the first hikers to reach the trailhead at Cronin's Yard, and as we packed our gear, another climber arrived and asked if he could join us. His name was Antonio Ulloa Reinoso, a medical doctor from Spain. We agreed, and the three of us set out up the lower slopes of the mountain to the most difficult part, a section called the Devil's Ladder. It is a steep, narrow gully filled with loose rock and boulders. We scrambled up through the debris and emerged onto the broad saddle above. From there, an hour of hiking through more fog brought us to the summit, at 3,414 feet, crowned by a sixteen-foot-tall cross that was placed there in 1950. There were enough gaps in the clouds that we were able to get brief views down into the green valleys around us.

Antonio's English was limited, so I found it interesting to travel all the way to Ireland to climb and speak Spanish. Antonio said, "This is like a miracle for me. I meet two expert climbers and one of them speaks Spanish. What good luck." Antonio specializes in teaching medical classes for search and rescue responders. He is also in the middle of a personal quest—to reach the highest summits of all twenty-seven nations of the European Union. Carrauntoohil was the twelfth peak of his project.

He is a big soccer fan. Our trip to the British Isles coincided with the World Cup soccer tournament in South Africa, and because the United States had made it to the second round, many conversations during those days centered on how well England and the U.S. had done, and who might eventually win the World Cup. When both England and the U.S. lost in the second round, the tone changed, and newspapers reviewing England's performance touted headlines

A Journey Supporting The Rowell Fund

like ROUT OF AFRICA.

The day we climbed with Antonio, Spain was playing its neighbor Portugal that evening. Although we parted ways as Antonio left for the airport, John and I found ourselves in front of a TV later that day cheering for Spain because of our new friend. Then, after we had returned home and Spain won the World Cup, 1-0 over The Netherlands, I emailed Antonio congratulations for his country's success, and we received a friendly reply that relived the memories of our day together on Ireland's highpoint.

The final climb for the Top of the British Isles expedition was Slieve Donard (Sleeve DON-ard), south of Belfast in Northern Ireland. We parked in Newcastle, just one hundred and fifty yards from the Irish Sea, and hiked in fog as heavy as that on Ben Nevis; however, Slieve Donard added the challenge of high winds of up to fifty miles per hour as we reached the high ridge leading to the summit.

Just before we started up the ridge, we met two Irish climbers who were traversing several peaks that day. We had seen the long stone wall that followed the spine of the ridge, so I asked one of the climbers what it was. He explained that it defined the division of the watershed. He acknowledged that such a marker was insignificant, but that the government had designed the project to provide jobs for people in hard times, perhaps like the Civilian Conservation Corps projects in the United States.

We had grown used to being questioned as soon as people heard our American accents. One of the two Irish climbers asked where we were from and I said, "The United States." He said, "I got that. Which state?" We told him Colorado and Montana, and he, like many others, talked about the beauty of the Rocky Mountains.

The four-foot stone wall on the ridgeline proved helpful. We stayed to the downwind side of it and protected ourselves from the strong gusts. We could hear the winds whistling through the stones, but the wall was just high enough to keep us from getting blasted. By the time we reached the summit, the wind was up to about seventy mph. With the loose footing and force of the wind, we staggered onto the summit and had to brace ourselves to remain standing in one spot. We shot video and still photos of each other struggling to hold onto the American flag as the fierce winds threatened to rip it from our hands and toss it into the Irish Sea. That wind, combined with the dense fog, steady rain, and poor visibility, gave an eerie sense to our final climb.

"Without a doubt, my favorite peak was Slieve Donard in Northern Ireland," John said. "Not because it was the highest, which it isn't, or had the most dramatic views, which we had virtually none. It was because of the weather on the summit. The hurricane-force winds, the rain whipping horizontally and Steve leaning into the gale yelling, 'Is that all you've got?' was a snapshot in time that will stay with me forever. We were like kids having fun in the most miserable weather conditions."

We were happy to drop back down out of the high wind, and by the time we returned to Newcastle, we were bathed in sunshine. We spent the afternoon sitting on the boardwalk, watching the waves, and eating fish and chips. There was something perfect about that moment. We had been flying, driving or climbing every day for ten days. At that point, there was nowhere left to go, no mountains left to climb. We had succeeded on all five highpoints and had had fun, in spite of heavy fog on every peak. We had talked earlier about spending the afternoon in Belfast, but after the raging wind on the summit of Slieve Donard, sitting on the benches at the boardwalk was so peaceful, so calm, that neither one of us suggested getting back in the car and driving again. We watched the waves for an hour. Two hours. Three hours. We talked about the hikes we had done. We remembered other climbs from past years. We dreamed of future peaks we would like to try. At that point, John and I had been climbing together for fourteen years.

While we might have wished for fewer clouds and better views from the summits, the five peaks had given us 16,200 feet of vertical gain/loss in nine calendar days. Those days left us with a sense of beauty, memories of wonderful people, and a renewed commitment to our highpointing for The Rowell Fund for Tibet.

Chapter 10

The Top of Scandinavia
July 2, 2011

One of my favorite exploration books is *Farthest North* by Fridtjof Nansen. The Norwegian hoped to be the first to reach the North Pole and devised an ingenious method of getting there. He heard about a ship that had wrecked off the coast of Siberia in the early 1880s. Pieces of that ship showed up a few years later on the northern coast of Greenland. Others had surmised that there was a natural drift in the Arctic sea ice, and Nansen wondered if he could use that drift to his advantage. While that idea germinated in his head, he set out with a team of six, and in 1888, they became the first to cross the Greenland ice cap on cross country skis. After the crossing, they were forced to winter over, which gave them seven months to study the methods of the local villagers. The information helped Nansen understand survival in the Arctic.

Following the Greenland trip, Nansen determined to make an attempt to reach the North Pole using the drift of the sea ice. He designed a unique wooden ship, the *Fram,* whose strong sides and rounded hull would allow it to rise upward as the sea ice froze around it. Nansen intended to intentionally strand his ship in the sea ice north of Siberia and ride the sea ice drift across the North Pole and out the other side near Greenland or Franz Joseph Land. He loaded *Fram* (which means Forward) with food and equipment for a five-year stay on the sea ice.

Thousands of adventurers applied for the twelve spots on the team, so Nansen had his pick of the best men available. Many people doubted the sanity of his idea, but Nansen was convinced he could succeed and departed in June 1893. By late September, he ordered the engines shut down and the *Fram* was encased in the sea ice. As predicted, the round hull allowed the ship to rise and settle on top of the ice. The long wait began.

At first the progress was frustrating. The ice moved east and west, then south. At one point they were farther south than when they started, but then the movement north began. Nansen carefully monitored his team's progress as they reached 84 degrees four minutes north, a new record. However, by March 1895, he realized the path he had chosen, while heading north, was going to miss the North Pole. He had to create another solution. On March 14, he and Hjalmar Johanson left the *Fram* on skis and dog sleds to attempt to reach the North Pole on foot. This worked well until April 7, when Nansen realized that they would have to turn back or risk being too far north when the sea ice broke up for the summer. After reaching 86 degrees, 13.6 minutes north, Nansen and Johanson turned back and traveled to Franz Joseph Land, an archipelago north of Scandinavia, where they spent the winter in a hut of stones and moss.

In the spring, they set out using two kayaks they had carried from the *Fram* and on June 17, 1895, they were attacked by a walrus. While they stopped to repair the damage, Nansen heard a dog bark. When he walked the coast to investigate, he ran into the British explorer Frederick Jackson, who was leading an expedition to Franz Joseph Land. Nansen and Johanson joined Jackson's ship and returned to Norway.

In the meantime, the *Fram* had drifted across the Arctic Ocean and was released into open water. The crew made their way to Tromso, Norway, where they were reunited with Nansen and Johanson, and the full team returned to Oslo (called Christiania at that time) on September 9, 1895. Thousands of people turned out at the harbor to welcome the team home. Nansen and his crew were national heroes. His fame and legacy would soon grow even bigger.

A Journey Supporting The Rowell Fund 101

With that story of Nansen in my mind, I was very excited to visit his homeland during our 2011 Top of Scandinavia trip and the highpoints of Denmark, Sweden, Finland, and Norway.

When John and I had climbed Carrauntoohil in Ireland the previous summer with Antonio Reinoso, he had talked about the beauty of Kebnekaise in Sweden. He said it was his favorite peak in his quest to reach the highpoints of the European Union. That sparked our interest in Scandinavia.

While the Top of the British Isles trip had just been two of us, John wanted more friends and family along for Scandinavia. Joining us would be Terri Baker, David Baker and Jessica Morse, along with Kevin Allison, Joe Sears and his daughter Samantha, and my youngest daughter Denby.

We started off on June 28 with an easy highpoint in Denmark: Mollehoj (MOW-ya-hoy), a three-hour drive outside Copenhagen and a five-minute walk from the parking lot. The highpoint is marked by a stone millwheel near a barn.

From Copenhagen, we took a high-speed train to Stockholm,

The Top of Scandinavia team gathers in the Oslo, Norway, airport before their return to the United States.. The group succeeded in reaching the highpoints of Denmark, Sweden, Finland, and Norway. From left, Denby Gardiner, Jessica Morse, Kevin Allison, David Baker, Terri Baker, Steve Gardiner, John Jancik, and Joe Sears. Photo courtesy of John Jancik.

a city built on fourteen islands connected by a maze of bridges, and explored Gamla Stan, the oldest district in Stockholm, before driving north fifteen hours to Kiruna (KEER-oo-na). On the way, the highway crossed the Arctic Circle, so we stopped the cars and celebrated what was for John, Terri, Joe and me, our third trip north of that latitude. We had flown across it in 1996 and 2001 on our trips to northern Greenland, but this was the first time we had driven across the noted line.

As we drove into Kiruna, I remembered that a high school English teacher had arranged for each student in his class to have a pen pal. Mine had been a girl from Kiruna, Sweden. Like most pen-pal experiences of the day, the exchange lasted two or three letters and was forgotten. I wondered if she still lived in Kiruna and chuckled how tiny bits of life sometimes weave themselves together.

On July 1, we drove to Nikkaluokta, the trailhead for Kebnekaise. We knew this highpoint would be the most difficult of the trip. It

On the Top of Scandinavia Expedition, John Jancik (left) and Steve Gardiner are dwarfed by the glaciers and cliffs of Kebnekaise, the highpoint of Sweden. The impressive snow pyramid of the summit, which lies almost 100 miles north of the Arctic Circle, is clearly visible in the upper left.
Photo by Jessica Morse.

requires a twelve-mile hike into the mountain lodge, a long summit day, and a hike out on the third day. We were worried about the low clouds and light rain on the approach hike, and hoped for better weather on summit day.

When we reached the mountain lodge, we had dinner, then a team meeting. We discussed the possible routes on the mountain. Everyone wanted to climb the East Ridge, which contains a section called the via ferrata. It is a high-angle, exposed section of rock protected by a steel cable running through bolts drilled into the mountain. It sounded fun, but any problem with the weather or a teammate who was sick or unable to climb the route would likely end the climb for everyone. In the end, the team decided to climb up the via ferrata and go down the other side of the mountain, completing a traverse across a second summit called Vierranvarri (VEER-an-var-ee). I was anxious about the decision. We had traveled so far to climb this mountain, I wanted us to have the best chance of success. I kept thinking about the low clouds in the afternoon. One thing that gave me more confidence, however, was the Arctic summer sun.

"There is something almost mystical about hiking and climbing in an area above the Arctic Circle where there is twenty-four-hour daylight," Joe said. "Under these conditions, time of day no longer matters. One is able to carry out an agenda based on stamina and conditions rather than the amount of available daylight."

I was still nervous. On the other hand, if we could successfully climb the via ferrata and traverse the second peak, it would be a superb day. I didn't sleep well that night, and it wasn't just the daylight at midnight.

We had seen earlier that the first section of the climb before we reached the glaciers would be steep trail and loose rock, what climbers often call a "grunt." Hard work, slow progress, lots of perspiration.

It took us three hours to put that sweaty section behind us, and I just hoped the via ferrata went well, so we did not have to go back down the steep section in depressed moods.

When we met the first snowfield, we put on our gaiters, crampons and harnesses, and unpacked our ice axes. We then traversed across to our left toward the Bjorlings Glacier. The traverse was steep, a good warmup to the exposed climbing we would face above. We crossed the Bjorlings Glacier to the base of a sharp snow ridge leading to the via ferrata. It was time to rope everyone together.

Other groups had climbed the route in recent days, so we were able to use their footsteps in the snow. That made it much easier to climb. We were staying right on the prow of the ridge, so the snow dropped off quickly on both sides of us.

"Dad, I am not sure about this," Denby said. This was the steepest snow she had ever climbed.

"That's why I tied you on the rope right behind me," I replied. "Just focus on putting your foot in each step. Move smoothly and stay focused."

We were two hundred feet up the spine of snow, so there was reason for concern. I watched her take a few steps. She looked good, relaxed. She was a college swimmer at the time, so she understood the meaning of focus, and she translated it well to the climbing. We moved intently up the final one hundred feet of the snow and found a flat spot to rest. The via ferrata began just to our right where the snow ridge met the rock face.

I stopped and Denby walked to me. With the snow ridge behind her, she smiled. She had faced the self-doubt that every climber experiences. She had overcome that doubt and knew she could climb the rest of Kebnekaise.

The others followed and stood on the flat spot. We drank water and looked at the via ferrata. Most importantly, we looked at the sky. The low clouds from the day before were gone. The sky was solid blue, unblemished. It was a day created for climbing.

We climbed the via ferrata still roped together, using a sling-and-carabiner system to keep us attached to the steel cable and bolts. We moved in unison up the blocky route, finding plenty of handholds and footholds to keep moving. We made good progress and enjoyed the views of the glaciers below and blue sky above.

About two-thirds of the way up the via ferrata, I stopped and

A Journey Supporting The Rowell Fund

tied myself to a bolt anchor on a roomy ledge. Joe had volunteered to climb in the back, and he had plenty of leading experience, so I decided it would be good to pause the group, let everyone catch their breath, and then let Joe lead on past us, reversing the order of everyone on the rope. We made the switch easily, and Joe led to the top of the via ferrata where it meets the broad upper slope of Kebnekaise. There, we removed the rope and climbed easily up to the summit pyramid.

The broad slope is rocky and the summit pyramid is a snowy, white fang piercing the blue sky. At the base of the snow, we dropped our backpacks. We would not need them or any equipment for the fifteen-minute hike up the snow to the summit. The final steps to the summit were airy, a sharp ridge of snow dropping off steeply on both sides, no place to become complacent and make a mistake.

At the top, we took photos and admired a wide view of Sweden. After several minutes on top, we climbed down to our backpacks, ate a good lunch, and set off toward the saddle between Kebnekaise and Vierranvarri.

Stepping carefully, Steve Gardiner (left), Denby Gardiner, and Jessica Morse traverse a steep snowfield on the approach to the Via Ferrata on Kebnekaise in Sweden.
Photo by John Jancik.

There was no trail down to the saddle, so it was a delicate piece of rock-hopping and side-stepping to get down to the saddle, where we filled our water bottles and hiked thirty minutes to the top of Vierranvarri. For years, it has been a tradition that each group builds a rock cairn on the flat top of Vierranvarri. Hundreds of cairns rise into a geological forest. We added a small one of our own.

Hiking down the valley below Vierranvarri, we came across a stream with no bridge. Normally it would have been an easy hop across it, but the hot sun of the day had melted more snow than usual, and the stream was swollen. We searched for many minutes, both upstream and downstream, before finding a reasonable way to cross it.

We arrived at the mountain lodge fourteen hours after we left it.
Tired.
Sore feet.
Happy.

Kebnekaise had challenged us all. "It started with the six-hour hike in, continuing on up the East Route the second day with glaciers and crevasses," Jessica said. "The most challenging part mentally was the via ferrata as well as finally making it to the tiny snowy summit that was intimidating but so beautiful and gratifying. It was a hike and view I hope I never forget."

At the lodge, John talked to one of the local climbing guides. The guide said there are usually only two or three days each year as perfect as the one we had on Kebnekaise.

"Kebnekaise was a classic climb featuring a wide variety of types of climbing," John said. "The mountain's exposed summit pyramid was especially dramatic and put an exclamation point on the wonderful ascent."

The next morning was slow. We ate. We talked. We packed. It was eleven a.m. before we managed to pull together enough energy to leave the lodge and hike out.

The twelve-mile walk gave us a chance to think about the beauty of Kebnekaise and the experience of climbing it. Jessica said, "I

A Journey Supporting The Rowell Fund 107

(Left). Terri Baker, left, and her daughter Jessica Morse, share a windy ride on a ferry across a fjord in Norway. Photo by John Jancik.

(Below). John Jancik (left), Joe Sears, and Steve Gardiner (kneeling) celebrate on the summit of Kebnekaise, one of their favorite highpoint ascents. Photo by Jessica Morse.

remember feeling so happy about all of our accomplishments."

Joe added, "It was wonderful to be back together with many of the same individuals that have participated in the Top of the World, Top of Africa, and 50 for Tibet expeditions, and to climb with three new adventurous people that share the same energy and drive to visit new places. Every mountain we have climbed on past expeditions has presented its unique challenges and vistas. This trip was no exception."

We drove four hours from Kiruna, Sweden, to Kilpisjarvi (KEEL-pees-yar-vee), Finland. Herds of reindeer lined the highway and often wandered onto it. A small herd roamed the hotel parking lot. With the reindeer and the midnight sun, we knew we had truly arrived in the far north.

The next day, July 4, was our only scheduled day off. John had learned that it was possible to take a boat ride on Kilpisjarvi Lake to a dock on the far side, hike a short distance, and see the tri-point marker where the borders of Finland, Sweden, and Norway meet. It sounded like a relaxing way to spend the day, so we took the boat ride and made the short hike. The tri-point marker is in the middle of a smaller lake, so there is a boardwalk out to and around a bright yellow marker.

We walked around the marker, visited with a Swedish man who was biking 4,000 kilometers from northern Norway to southern Sweden, and returned to the dock to await the boat. As the boat left the dock, we heard clunking sounds below, and soon the boat stopped. Black smoke poured out of the hold. (In a bit of dramatic irony, at the same moment that Denby and I watched black smoke fill the boat we were on, at home in Montana, my wife Peggy was watching black smoke pour out of the next-door neighbor's house, which was gutted by the fire.)

The captain crawled down into the hold and returned. "This has never happened before," he said. One female passenger seemed distraught. "When will be start moving?" she asked. "I have a dinner reservation." The captain paused, then said, "I am doing what I can."

He called a fishing boat on the radio. They showed up in minutes and tied a rope onto the front of the tour boat, a humorous vision because the tour boat was at least ten times larger than the fishing boat. The fishing boat struggled to pull the tour boat, but quickly ran out of gas. More than one joke was made about *Gilligan's Island* and the scheduled three-hour tour.

The captain called the rescue service and an hour later, they showed up, filled the fishing boat with gas, and tied both boats to the tour boat. Waves were building in front of a strong wind. By the time the two boats pulled us to town, the water was so choppy that they could not take the tour boat to the dock. The smaller boats had to ferry passengers two or three at a time to the shore. We had been stalled for three hours. The woman had already missed her dinner reservation.

The highpoint of Finland offered a unique adventure. Halti (HALL-tee) is 4,355 feet in elevation and is located in Lapland one hundred miles north of the Arctic Circle. It is a moderate, yet intimidating peak, as the normal climbing route requires six days' round trip. We shortened that distance and added a splash of adventure by picking up a float plane in Kilpisjarvi and flying twenty-five minutes into a lake near the base of Halti on July 5. The plane was very narrow, with only four seats. With the pilot occupying one seat, our group of eight needed three flights in and three flights out.

At eight a.m. our first group of David, Kevin, and Terri left for Halti. The pilot, Hakki, shuttled back to pick up John, Jessica, and Joe in the second flight, and Denby and me for the third flight.

Kevin Allison from Centennial, Colorado, recalled the flight in the floatplane as "an opportunity to witness the extent of the Arctic wilderness and the powerful imprint of glaciers on the landscape."

I had imagined landing on a lake in a floatplane would be very soft, but was surprised that it was much rougher than I expected. The pontoons chattered on the waves, much like water skiing outside the wake of a boat.

Since our three groups were separated by nearly an hour, each group walked up the valley toward Halti on their own, wanting to make sure we had everyone back down for the return flights in the evening.

While Denby and I were walking and talking, I heard a sound like low voices talking. I stopped to listen. It seemed to be coming from the hill above us. I got out my binoculars and could see two or three hundred reindeer near the top of the hill. They were grazing and had blended into the hillside so completely that we had not seen them farther away.

When we had climbed the state highpoint in Connecticut, we learned that it was on the side of Mount Frissell and the actual summit of the mountain was in Massachusetts. A similar setup exists in Finland. The Finnish highpoint is on the side of Halti and the summit is a two-minute walk into Norway.

Our three groups reached the highpoint on Halti separately. The second group of Joe, John, and Jessica were moving the fastest, so they left Halti and opted to climb a second peak nearby, the highest mountain completely within the border of Finland. The group of Terri, David, and Kevin decided to climb Halti and return to the lake to meet the floatplane. Denby and I decided to do the same.

John had found the moment on top of Halti a special treat. "To think we were on the northernmost international highpoint on Earth was a pretty neat feeling to have."

The two other groups had already left the summit when Denby and I arrived, so we had a few minutes to ourselves at both the highpoint of Finland and the summit of Halti. I couldn't help but think about the time I spent with Romney on Kilimanjaro. Denby's trip with our group had been much more relaxed, more joyful. I was glad. One fearful trip in the mountains with a daughter is enough for any father.

Denby and I walked down from the 4,355-foot summit to a series of orange rocks lower on the mountain. They provided a flat, sunny spot to rest and lay in the sun. We ate a pleasant lunch together, then walked back down the valley to the dock to meet the floatplane. Joe, John, and Jessica were there, and as the floatplane arrived, we helped them load their packs and get settled in the plane. A strong wind was blowing, so the floatplane rocked against the dock. We had trouble getting it turned around and headed out to the lake, but managed, and Hakki took off for the return to Kilpisjarvi.

Chilled, Denby and I stacked our backpacks up a few yards away from the dock and huddled behind them. Hakki returned in forty-five minutes to pick us up. By then, Terri, David, and Kevin had arrived, so Terri joined Denby and me in the second return flight. David and Kevin caught the third flight, and with all of us back in Kilpisjarvi, we went to a restaurant to celebrate.

The countries of Finland, Sweden, and Norway are long and narrow. For a group with plans like ours, this means a lot of driving. With the Danish highpoint so far south, and the Finnish and Swedish highpoints so far north, we had some long days in cars.

From Halti in Finland, our group had a twenty-four-hour drive to Galdhøpiggen, the highpoint of Norway. "The two-day drive would have been excruciating if it weren't for the complete sense of awe every time I looked out the window," Jessica said. When the trip began, she thought, "What a great vacation this will be. Within the first couple of days, I realized this was far from a vacation, and it was most definitely an expedition. Crossing four countries in two weeks and hiking the four highpoints was no easy task, but I enjoyed it immensely."

I saw on the map that one section of the highway was designated a Scenic Route. I was looking forward to that, but soon realized that it looked just like the beautiful mountains and waterfalls we were seeing on every road in Norway. I decided they could call the entire country Norway National Park.

In the British Isles the previous summer, John and I had been plagued with heavy fog, occasional rain, and terrible visibility. Maybe it was Mother Nature's payback, but we had been extremely lucky with weather in Scandinavia. The weather again held perfect for the ascent of Galdhøpiggen, a seven-hour climb on precipitous, rocky terrain and snowfields. "The Norway highpoint was the most beautiful summit of the trip, in my opinion, and we were lucky to spend an entire hour on top enjoying it and eating our lunch in the sun," Jessica said.

That moment was important for everyone on the team. "Reaching the summit of Galdhøpiggen was certainly the culmination for the expedition. It is the highest point in Scandinavia and northern Europe," John said. "The route to the top that we chose was a 4,000-foot ascent but relatively straightforward. Galdhøpiggen's surrounding countryside was spectacular with heavily glaciated peaks stretching to the horizon. Many miles had been traveled, four country highpoints reached, and beautiful weather every summit day. We could not have asked for a better outcome to all the planning and training that went into the Top Of Scandinavia Expedition."

"My favorite memory of the trip was definitely the summits," Denby said. "Standing on those peaks and seeing the miles and miles of amazing landscape is such a reward for the long, rigorous, physical haul, and makes it more than worth it. The most fun for me was traveling with my dad and his friends and getting the opportunity to test my physical limits and to prove to myself that I was capable. It was great to be included in the 50 for Tibet group. This was a really positive part of my life."

Joe added, "Climbing the highpoints of three of the northernmost countries in the world is in itself a great adventure; however, it is pretty incredible that half of the individuals on this team have also been to the top of the northernmost mountain in the world (during the 2001 expedition to North Peary Land, Greenland). I would be willing to bet that this team is the only team in the world that can claim those feats."

After Galdhøpiggen, we spent one night in Lillehammer, home of the 1992 Winter Olympics, before driving into Oslo for the final day of the trip. As we drove to Oslo, my thoughts returned to Fridjof Nansen and his bold attempt to reach the North Pole by using the sea ice drift in the Arctic Ocean. After that expedition, he immediately wrote his classic book *Farthest North*, then resumed his scientific work at the Royal Frederick University, publishing six volumes of scientific work from his expedition. By the early 1900s, Norway's union with Sweden, forced in place by the Great Powers in 1814, was strained and Nansen wrote several newspaper articles supporting the separation which eventually came about in 1905. Nansen was appointed Norway's first minister to London and helped establish Norway's place in the world. By 1910, he gave his ship, the *Fram* to fellow Norwegian explorer Roald Amundsen who took the ship on an expedition to the South Pole. Nansen continued his scientific work, but was interrupted following World War I when he became president of Norway's League of Nations Society. In 1921, he accepted the post of the League of Nations High Commissioner for Refugees. He helped relocate a half-million war prisoners and refugees with what became known as "Nansen Passports," work that led to him receiving the Nobel Peace Prize in 1922. He died of a heart attack in 1930.

As we drove to Oslo, I knew I wanted to visit the Nobel Prize museum and see the display for Fridjof Nansen. However, while in Norway, we also learned that the *Fram* was located in a museum in Oslo. I hoped I would have a chance to see the famous ship.

In Oslo, we were able to visit a museum of Viking ships as well as the museum for the *Kon Tiki*, the raft that Norwegian explorer Thor Heyerdahl used to travel from Peru to Polynesia in 1947. Nearby was the museum for the *Fram*.

I was excited to see it, and hoped that perhaps we could get close enough to touch it. I was shocked when we walked into the building large enough to hold the ship and saw the stairway leading up to the main deck. We walked on board. We looked up at the masts, grabbed hold of the ship's wheel, walked down the steps to see the kitchen and crew quarters, and wandered through every inch of the ship. I looked around and imagined Nansen, Sverdrup and Amundsen calling this ship home. To think of the polar history, both Arctic and Antarctic, and the people who lived on the *Fram* left me with a deep sense of awe.

Having left the sleeping huts at Station 8 at three thirty a.m., Steve Gardiner admires the first light of day on the upper slopes of Mount Fuji in Japan.
Photo by John Jancik.

Chapter 11

The Top of Japan
August 1, 2012

It is one of the most photographed mountains on earth. Its symmetrical volcanic cone reaches high into the clouds some 60 miles southwest of Tokyo.

It is Mount Fuji, the 12,389-foot legendary highpoint of Japan, and it became the next goal for the 50 for Tibet project.

"The mountain dominates the landscape," John said. "It has no foothills. The crater at the top is very impressive and deep. It is an active volcano last erupting in 1708. This is a reminder of the live geology that is in Japan, just like the tragic earthquake they had in 2011."

On that dramatic mountain, our ascent would result in many emotions—determination, concern, amazement, joy, and unfortunately, sadness.

The journey to the highest mountain in Japan had been the idea of ECHO Geophysical employee Cindy Early, Terri Baker's sister. Cindy had lived in Japan for two years in the 1980s and suggested the trip to John, who liked the idea and began putting together a twelve-person team.

"Hiking to the top of Mount Fuji seems like a natural extension of what 50 for Tibet had accomplished domestically and internationally over the previous six years," John said. "Promoting the cultural and artistic aspects of the Tibetans is a worldwide cause deserving of the spotlight as often as possible, wherever possible. Many Japanese are Buddhist, although most belong to sects which are not direct followers of Tibetan Buddhism and the Dalai Lama."

Cindy was excited to return to Japan and share the Japanese culture with her friends and family. Although she did not climb Mount Fuji when she lived in Japan, to do so with the 50 for Tibet project "represents both physical and spiritual journeys. In preparation for climbing Fuji San, I am working out to be in the best physical shape I can," she said. "I am vigorously brushing up my Japanese language skills. I am excited to visit my Japanese friends, eat wonderful food, and have linguistic adventures."

The trip was scheduled to leave on June 30.

However, Cindy became seriously ill and unexpectedly passed away on June 15. It was a devastating time for family, friends, and the Top of Japan team.

The team ultimately became more determined to climb Mount Fuji and postponed the trip until July 28. Cormac Dorsey, also an employee of ECHO Geophysical and Cindy's husband, joined the team and decided to have a memorial service to Cindy on the summit of Mount Fuji.

In addition to Cormac, the team included John and Terri, David Baker, his father Dave Baker, his wife Kathy Baker, Jessica Morse, Jacob Artz, Paul Konichek, Joe Sears, my wife Peggy, and me.

While Cindy lived in Japan, she "gained a deep appreciation and love of Japanese culture. Additionally she taught herself to read, write, and speak Japanese," Cormac said. "Cindy and I got married in 1984. We took a three-month honeymoon traveling around the world headed west. This included visiting Japan. Over the years we returned to Japan. We also had Japanese children come and stay in our home to experience life in the United States. Our friend Hiroko came a few times. One goal for her was to perfect her English. With Cindy's coaching, she took first place in the All-Japan Inter-Middle School English Oratorical Contest."

A Journey Supporting The Rowell Fund

Our delayed expedition left the United States on July 28 and landed in Tokyo on July 29. The team took a day to recover from the travel and jet lag as well as see Tokyo before taking a bus to Mount Fuji on July 30. We left the Kawaguchi 5th Station early in the afternoon and followed the Yoshida Route toward the summit of Fuji. The route is a well-developed trail with many switchbacks and retaining walls to protect climbers from rockfall.

The weather in the days prior to our ascent had been rainy, but the two days we were on the mountain were clear and dry. "The weather was wonderful," said John. "We had a lucky window of time because that trail would be very slick in rain. Our good luck with weather from last summer in Scandinavia seemed to have stuck with us."

First climbed in 700 AD by Buddhist monk En-no-Shokaku, Mount Fuji is a pilgrimage site for many Japanese, so the climbing routes can be crowded each day during the short season in July and August. So many people climb it that each route has an up trail and a down trail. Both are in constant use throughout the day and night.

"I read that there can be as many as eight thousand people on the mountain during the high season," John said. "It is more of a spiritual or cultural experience than a wilderness experience. It should not be underestimated, however, because the weather can be volatile, there is no official rescue option, and the mountain is over twelve thousand feet elevation."

Jessica Morse, who had also been on the trip to Scandinavia, said, "Climbing with hundreds of other people was very different. Though it was frustrating standing around and waiting at times, it was special to see so many people ranging in age from young to old climbing and all having a common goal."

With so many hikers on the mountain, local venders have set up stores at small stations located about one or two hours climb apart. The stores sell food, drink and supplies that hikers might need. Most of the stations also offer bunk beds because the climb is more than most people can accomplish in one day. It is possible to hike the mountain from the bottom beginning at Station 1, but most climbers start at Station 5, as we did, where the bus terminal is located.

Our team climbed throughout the afternoon, up the steep series of switchbacks to Station 8. With night approaching, we decided to rent bunks in the shelter. We had a cup of tea in the cafe, then crowded ourselves in, side by side, on the long bunks, and went to bed early to prepare for the three thirty a.m. start toward the summit. With many other groups coming in and out of the hut, our sleep was intermittent.

As Peggy and I walked up the trail together, we enjoyed commenting on the ever-changing views of the landscape and the winding trail stretched out below us. At three thirty, we were less talkative, but the few hours of rest had left us ready for the final hike to the summit.

By five thirty, we watched as the rising sun highlighted clouds below us. At one point, Peggy, Joe Sears, and I stopped and sat on some large rocks, viewing the morning lightshow.

From there, we finished the hike to the crater rim, arriving at the top about seven a.m. "The climb was difficult for me, yet very satisfying," Peggy said. "It was exciting to get to the top and look around. It was a challenge to push myself to get to the top, but it was good to know that the work we put in before we left paid off."

At the crater rim, even more venders have set up shop. We took a quick walk through the area, but as soon as all of our group reached the rim, we walked to a flat area closer to the crater and away from the shop crowds.

Cormac and other family members held a memorial to Cindy. Holding hands and facing the crater of Mount Fuji, they took turns talking about Cindy's life, her connection to Japan, and their memories of her.

"When Cormac kneeled down and began to spread some of Cindy's ashes, tears welled up in my eyes," John said. "It was quite an emotional moment to watch. I believe Cindy was also there in spirit and watching over us as we celebrated her life in a land so significant to her."

Cormac later explained, "Mount Fuji has a special importance in Japanese culture. It was so great to be able to celebrate and honor Cindy's life in such an amazing place. I appreciate the support and camaraderie from everyone on the team."

Paul Konichek, John's brother-in-law from Wisconsin Rapids, Wisconsin, called Cindy the thirteenth member of the team and the force that "held us all together in order to drive the expedition forward to its completion. Another most unbelievable chapter in the 50 for Tibet cause is now a loving memory of Cindy Early and the highpoint of the country she loved and loved her back."

After the ceremony, Joe, Cormac, Jessica, and John elected to walk around the crater rim and the rest chose to begin the long descent. While the up route had many switchbacks, the down route was more direct and the boots of descending climbers raised clouds of dust. Dave Baker called the trail "lava marbles," and many hikers ended up on the seat of their pants. Though the trail was loose and

On the crater rim of Mount Fuji in Japan, Cormac Dorsey (second from right) remembers the life of his wife Cindy Early who passed away just before the Top of Japan trip. Cormac is joined by family members Dave Baker, Kathy Baker, Jacob Artz, Jessica Morse, David Baker, and John Jancik.
Photo by Steve Gardiner.

slippery, it let us drop quickly down the mountain, and we returned to Station 5 and the bus terminal by noon. We caught the one p.m. bus back to Tokyo in a light rain. We were a tired, dusty group that boarded that bus, but we agreed that it had been a big experience to complete a hike that means so much to the Japanese people.

From Tokyo, we took the bullet train to Kyoto, the ancient capital of Japan, "a charming city with cultural and spiritual significance located in a basin of tree-lined hills," John said.

To get a deeper sense of Japanese history, we visited the Imperial Palace, Kiyamizu Temple, Honen-In Temple, Nishi-Honganji Temple, and strolled the Philosopher's Walk. Because all the street signs were only in Japanese, we had to be careful of where we were walking and keep track of how to get back to the hotel, because we could not pronounce its name. We took a business card from the hotel desk so we could show it to taxi drivers when we needed to return. We also used a guidebook and showed the drivers the page in the guidebook to steer them to a temple or market.

"Visiting the temples and shrines in Kyoto was amazing," Peggy said. "The beauty and sense of calmness they brought was wonderful. We were also lucky enough to see geisha girls in their full makeup and dress."

In Kyoto, the team stayed at a ryokan, a traditional Japanese hotel, arranged by friends of Cindy Early. "I was most impressed with the ryokan we stayed at in Kyoto," said Jessica. "I enjoyed being able to experience true tradition and culture by sleeping on bed rolls on tatami mats, Japanese bathing, and Japanese eating."

Cindy's idea to take our 50 for Tibet project to Mount Fuji in Japan had been a good one. Her memorial ceremony had been a powerful moment for us all. It was a chance to reflect on our families, our lives, and our project, as well. Since 2006, the 50 for Tibet project had reached the summits of forty-eight state highpoints and the District of Columbia, as well as ten international highpoints and had raised over $250,000 to support Tibetan artists, writers, musicians and others through The Rowell Fund for Tibet. Our efforts were paying off and making a significant impact.

The successful ascent of Mount Fuji also meant that John and Joe, the May 19 birthday boys, and I had climbed mountains together on five continents.

Those journeys had been opportunities for all kinds of adventures. We had met many interesting people. Six-year-old Tommy, hiking with his dad on Mount Frissell in Connecticut, was so happy to be out walking on the trail, and he was really excited when John let him sign the Galen Rowell book. He was learning to appreciate the outdoors and active sports, an important trait, especially in today's screen-watching, sedentary society. In the upper section of Tuckerman's Ravine on Mount Washington, we talked to a man from Colorado. When we told him about our project, he said, "I have heard about what you are doing. I read about it in the *Rocky Mountain News*." On Boundary Peak in Nevada, we met a woman who was climbing many of the western state highpoints alone. On Mount Elbert in Colorado, we talked to a girl who was climbing the mountain on her eighth birthday with her family, and soon after, met a man from Louisiana who said he was seventy-two. "I go a bit slower now," he said in his Southern drawl, "but I will get there eventually." We met scores of hikers who were doing the highpoint of their own state. Other hikers had a list of highpoints in their region. Some intended to reach the top of all fifty states. We met all kinds of people on the highpoints, and if we learned one thing from talking with so many of them, it would be that mean people don't go highpointing.

Traveling to and between highpoints was also a challenge. We had a flat tire in Arizona, and another in Hawaii. We encountered detours for road construction. Weather conditions made us change plans. Teammates got sick or had family emergencies. The arrangements were often cumbersome.

Bob Vite, from Denver, who went on the trip to Minnesota, Michigan, and Wisconsin, said, "It was incredible what it took to do those three small peaks. The logistics of getting there and putting the whole thing together to accomplish this were far greater than I ever expected. When I extrapolate that out to fifty state highpoints, I realize that this project is a huge commitment, and I am amazed at what they have done."

Vite said the long hours of driving and hiking were worth it. "The camaraderie that developed by being with those same people for three days created an interesting dynamic. It was an intense time, and we were close together for the whole trip."

Joe Sears agreed. "Some of these trips were very intense. We did so much in a short time. We were really moving, getting from one place to the next."

After the trip to Missouri and Louisiana, Cormac Dorsey said, "It was a great chance to meet people and travel through rural America. It really makes you aware of what a diverse country we have. Unless you travel you have no idea how different areas of the country are. I really thought the drive through Missouri was beautiful."

One thing we often talked about on the long drives was the idea that we were seeing roads, farms, towns, buildings, that we would never see without the highpointing project. On a road in Vermont, we stopped to buy maple syrup from a farmer's house. In Arkansas, we ate in a restaurant made from an old railroad boxcar. A Maine moose entertained us one afternoon by standing thigh-deep in a pond and

During the Top of Japan Expedition, Steve Gardiner, Peggy Gardiner, Jessica Morse, and Cormac Dorsey arrive at the small shops that mark the crater rim of Mount Fuji, one of Japan's "Three Holy Mountains."
Photo by John Jancik.

eating long strands of weeds. We waded in the Atlantic Ocean and a month later waded in the Pacific Ocean. I remember driving down a quiet backroad in Indiana and thinking, *I would never have seen this if not for coming to visit the state's highpoint.*

Highpointing comes in many forms. Some people have set out to climb the highest peak on all seven continents, a quest often called The Seven Summits, first completed by Dick Bass in 1985. Some people have climbed the highest points in each of the Canadian provinces. Others have traveled to the highpoints of each county within a given state. Our initial goal was the fifty states, but then we expanded our focus and added selected international country highpoints.

The first person known to highpoint all the states was Arthur H. Marshall, who finished in 1936 when there were only forty-eight states. The first to highpoint all fifty states was Vin Hoeman, who completed the task in 1966. Since then, two hundred and seventy-three people have reached all fifty state highpoints, and five hundred and twenty-four have reached the highpoints of the contiguous forty-eight states, according to the Highpointers Club. By comparison, more than 4,000 people have reached the summit of Mount Everest.

Because highpointing is gaining in popularity, it is normal to encounter other people on the trail or summit of any state highpoint. When we were on Mount Elbert in Colorado, at least forty other people were there with us. That made me think of an alternative project to highpointing—climbing the second highest peak in each state. It does not have the same flair as the highest point in each state, but it would be a unique project and few people would be on any of those landmarks.

While some of the summits we reached were true wilderness experiences, many were not, but that did not stop them from being an interesting day. The fact that dozens of state highpoints are accessible to people of all ages and physical abilities is also an attraction. Anyone with a car, a map, and one of the multiple guidebooks available can fill many days with enjoyable activity, see new sights, and meet interesting people.

After hiking the trail on Casamanya, Joe Sears was rewarded with views of almost all the mountains in the tiny nation of Andorra on the border between Spain and France.
Photo by Steve Gardiner.

Chapter 12

The Top of Iberia
July 5, 2013

Our 2001 Greenland quest to climb the northernmost mountain on earth taught us one thing—statistics about mountain climbing aren't as black-and-white as they might seem to be. We struggled with the definition of a mountain and spent endless hours discussing the difference between a rise, a mound, a hill, a mountain. Then, after weeks of exploring the northern coast of Greenland, we settled on the Three-Tooth Mountain near Sands Fjord as the northernmost.

Could someone dispute that claim using different definitions? Sure. Are there different definitions in countries around the world? Indeed.

So it was interesting that our goal in 2013, the Top of Iberia, involved us in two new discussions about mountain climbing measurements. The peaks of Spain, Portugal, and Andorra would provide us with physical challenges as well as geographic disputes as we continued to support the humanitarian work of The Rowell Fund for Tibet.

Although it seems that highpointing should be a simple endeavor (measure the peaks and the highest one wins), there are some subjective concerns that affect planning for these expeditions. Our 2013 excursion featured debates in both Spain and Portugal over whether the highpoint should be on the mainland of the country or if a higher point on an island owned by the country should count as the highpoint. We discussed this and in both cases, we chose to go after the actual highest peak owned by each country and add the adventure of hiking and climbing in the Azores Islands and Canary Islands.

"The unique experience of climbing in the Atlantic Ocean archipelago seemed like a real interesting option to our highpointing goals," John said.

As we planned the Iberian trip, Joe noted that "this group will be adding two more volcanoes to our list of highpoints and summits attained. For me, there is something fascinating about volcanoes. I think maybe its their imposing dominance over the surrounding landscape. Most volcanoes exhibit substantial vertical relief as solitary figures unimpeded by other nearby mountains. From every direction and every distance, there is a picture worth taking and remembering."

The highpoint on the mainland of Portugal is La Torre (6,539 feet), reached by a paved road and with a café on the summit. That did not seem very interesting; however, on Pico Island in the Azores, owned by Portugal, rises the higher summit, Pico Piquinho (7,713 feet). This mountain is a stratovolcano which features a large crater containing a second volcano inside the crater. The second pit volcano is higher than the crater rim, so our plan was to climb Pico to the crater rim, descend into the crater, then climb the interior volcanic cone, Pico Piquinho. It seemed like a fascinating challenge.

The Top of Iberia team consisted of John Jancik, Joe Sears, Sammy Sears, David Baker, Ashley Baker, Paul Konichek, Jessica Morse, Dan Giles, Peggy Gardiner, and me. We flew to Lisbon, Portugal, then caught a two-hour flight to Pico Island in the Azores. We were staying in Madelena, so we settled into our hotel, then took a walk around the village, ending up at a seaside restaurant for dinner. After dinner, we walked to the hotel in the dark, with a full moon highlighting the silhouette of Pico volcano. It dominates the island.

The next morning, June 23, we drove to the trailhead for Pico volcano. The ranger warned us that it was not a good day to climb the mountain. Pico was covered in fog, and he expected it may get worse. We could see the cloud layer, but it seemed clear above. We also knew that the climbing route contains forty-five white posts to help climbers on foggy days, much like the human-sized rock cairns that helped guide us through the thick fog on Ben Nevis in Scotland. We decided to start out and see how the conditions developed.

We had no trouble hiking, especially with the white posts giving us a sense of direction. The fog was hanging on the mountain, but not getting worse. The lower section of the route was green and easy, but it soon grew much steeper and turned to volcanic gravel. We slowed our pace and worked our way up through the steepest section until the angle eased back the last hour to the crater rim.

By the time we reached the crater, we had climbed above the clouds, so from the rim, we had a clear view into the crater and of the secondary volcanic cone inside. It looked like an excellent finishing

After climbing the volcano cone inside the larger volcano, John Jancik (left), Joe Sears, Paul Konichek, and Steve Gardiner reached the summit of Pico Piquenho in the Azores Islands. The nine islands, owned by Portugal, are in the west-central Atlantic Ocean. Photo by Sammy Sears.

climb. We climbed down a short distance into the crater, walked to the base of the smaller volcano, Pico Piquinho, and dropped much of our equipment there. We did not need the packs and the short climb up Pico Piquinho would be easier with less weight.

The route up the secondary volcanic cone was much steeper and began on rough blocks of volcanic rock. Near the top, the route moved inside a very high-angle chimney formed from an old lava tube, giving us sixty feet of really interesting climbing. At the top of the chimney, we turned to the right and faced the heat and smell of gas escaping from a small fumerole.

On the summit, we could see the full extent of the crater just below us, but beyond that, the cloud layer blocked any view of Pico Island or any of the other islands. We spent a few minutes there, then returned to the crater to retrieve our equipment and begin the descent.

The thick clouds we saw from the summit made the downclimb much more difficult. "There were times during the downclimb that we could not see more than forty feet in front of us," John said. "With multiple options branching off the route, we had to be very careful to stay on the main route. Given all that, there was a certain sense of beauty being on the volcano in a dense fog."

We were not able to see from one white post to another, so we left four of us at one white post while three others went ahead to locate the next white post. We then followed the trail the best we could and used voices to help with directions. It was a slower process, but an interesting hike and the clouds kept the temperature comfortable. Mist developed, adding to the unstable weather conditions, but fortunately, it did not turn into rain.

"What I remember most about Pico," Joe said, "is the aesthetics of the mountain. We started out in lush, green underbrush, then made the stark transition into the rocky volcanic region. The park ranger had warned us about the fog, but on the way up, it didn't seem much of a problem. The descent, however, was a huge challenge. One false move could have been bad."

Sharp downhill, like the middle section of Pico, is hard on a climber's feet. It often causes the toes to bump the front of the boots and that can get painful quickly. I could see that Peggy's feet were hurting her. She didn't complain about it, but I had seen that toe-pain walk with other climbers before and recognized what was going on. We slowed down, giving more time to place each foot and reduce any further damage.

She kept a steady pace back to the ranger station, where the ranger awarded each of us a certificate for successfully climbing Pico.

The next day, our flights back to Lisbon were in the evening, so we took the ferry to the nearby island of Horta and had beautiful views of Pico from the boat. It was exciting to know we had been to the top of such a magnificent peak and had seen the volcano inside the volcano. When the ferry arrived in Horta, we walked around the town, and returned to Pico in time for our flights. We had a nine-hour layover in Lisbon, so we found a seating area that was empty and spread out on the benches and slept until five-thirty a.m. and our flights to Madrid.

On June 28, we drove from Madrid to Andorra, a tiny nation of three mountain valleys, pinned between Spain and France in the Pyrenees Mountains. Home to only 85,000 people, the Principality of Andorra welcomes more than ten million tourists each year. They come to hike and ski in the nearby mountains and visit the stores and restaurants in the capital city of Andorra la Vella.

We hoped to climb Como Pedrosa (9,665 feet) outside the village of Arinsal, which features a 4,200-foot elevation gain and a full day of climbing through beautiful mountain scenery. To help us with final plans for our climb, we stopped in a mountaineering store on the main avenue in Andorra la Vella. Unfortunately, the information we got was all bad news.

It had been a high snow year, with more than twelve feet of snow on Coma Pedrosa. Even at the end of June, the snow was still deep and previous attempts to climb it had seen mixed results. We would need at least crampons and ice axes, but because it was midsummer, we had not brought any technical equipment with us and none was available for rent.

We had traveled this far, so we decided to go up into the valley, see the mountain, climb as high as we could, and then make our own judgment about the peak. We drove to the small village of Arinsal and hiked up the trail. We crossed two bridges which spanned scenic rivers, then set an easy pace up a steeper section of trail. Beyond that, the trail entered a side canyon where we found several patches of snow, but they were no problem. We hiked through this narrow canyon until it opened up into a small cirque with a waterfall and beautiful meadow. I stopped. That scene was beauty in its highest form. I stared. It was a moment of high energy and the power of nature mixing perfectly. I could vaguely hear the others moving on up the trail, but I stood. I couldn't move. I was captured by that scene, that moment.

We climbed one more section of rock and snow and entered a wide, long valley near the hiker's refuge. We could see the snow couloir across the valley. This was the main route to Coma Pedrosa, so

On the trail to Coma Pedrosa, Peggy Gardiner hikes in the afternoon sun of the Pyrenees Mountains of Andorra. Photo by Steve Gardiner.

we decided to get a closer look. We hiked up the broad valley and climbed to the snowline. Peggy and I decided to stop at that point while Joe, John, Dan, Paul, and Sammy continued higher. The route above curved to the right around a ridge and angled toward the summit of Coma Pedrosa, so they quickly moved out of our sight.

Peggy and I sat on flat rocks for several minutes, then walked back down to the refuge to eat lunch. We were just about ready to hike down when Joe called on the radio. They had climbed up the snow to a rough area of rocks and ice. Too dangerous. They had turned around.

"I climbed up the rocks in the couloir," Joe later remembered, "but I could see that getting the whole group, with various levels of experience, up the couloir might work well, but I was afraid that trying to get the group down would be much more difficult. If anyone had slipped in there, it would not be a good deal. I didn't want anyone to get hurt. It was in our best interest to go back down."

With Coma Pedrosa in bad shape for the season, we opted for a secondary plan. When we were getting information in the climbing store, the clerk had told us about another peak, Pico Casamanya, which would be clear, even in this high-snow year. She described the route to us, and we decided to try that.

The trail headed up through a forest, then broke out into open space after an hour of hiking. We followed a trail that switchbacked up a rocky slope to a summit that gave us views of the entire country of Andorra. We could easily pick out Coma Podrosa to the west and that view of the highpoint and its surrounding mountains made it clear why we had had so much trouble in that long and beautiful valley. So much snow covered the peaks of the Coma Podrosa region that few ridges, cliffs, or other features were visible. The peaks looked formidable. Hard as it had been to leave Coma Podrosa, it had clearly been the right decision.

We drove two days south along the Costa Brava and the Mediterranean Sea, stopping overnight to enjoy the beach at Alicante, before driving to Gibraltar. The Rock of Gibraltar, while not an official international highpoint (Gibraltar is a British Overseas Territory), is such a unique feature that we wanted to visit it to see the variety of caves and military installments. We hiked up the trail toward O'Hara's Battery, the highest point. Dan and Jessica had walked ahead of the rest of us, and when we arrived at the top, Jessica was smiling and showing off her new engagement ring. Dan had proposed to her on the Rock of Gibraltar.

"Getting engaged on top of the Rock of Gibraltar was a surreal moment," Jessica said. "It is known as one of the two pillars of Hercules and signifies strength, solidity, safety. I can't think of a better place to make a commitment to a person who has been my pillar."

From the highpoint, we walked down to St. Michael's Cave to tour the cave and see the concert hall built inside. We also walked to see the siege tunnels built in 1782. They had been an ingenious plan to protect not only the Rock of Gibraltar, but the entire narrow entrance to the Mediterranean Sea.

We had hoped to make a day trip to Tangier, Morocco, yet were concerned because high waves on the sea had prevented the ferry from crossing for six days in a row. We were lucky again when we learned the ferry could make the crossing the next morning. We were able to tour the beaches, ride a camel, and walk through the narrow, winding streets of the Kasbah (old fortress) and Medina (old city). We stopped in a market where Peggy bargained for jewelry for our daughters. She made a deal that ended up costing me my wristwatch.

Like Portugal, Spain has identified a highpoint on the mainland: Mulhacen (11,413 feet), in southern Spain, not far from the city of Grenada. We decided to go after the higher summit of Mount Teide (12,198) on Tenerife in the Canary Islands off the west coast of Africa.

Mount Teide is a national park, so access to the summit is controlled with climbers needing a permit that not only specifies the day but the time. Our permits were for eleven a.m., but we arrived at the park entrance almost an hour early. Other climbers had not

A Journey Supporting The Rowell Fund

Jessica Morse shows off her engagement ring moments after Dan Giles proposed to her atop the Rock of Gibraltar.
Photo by John Jancik.

shown up, so the attendant allowed us to enter early. Within forty-five minutes, our entire group was on the highpoint of Spain, looking out over what Joe described as a "moonscape."

With successful climbs of Pico Piquenho, Mount Teide, and the Rock of Gibraltar, and memories of a beautiful valley on our attempt of Coma Podrosa, our Top of Iberia trip was over. As teachers, Peggy and I were on summer vacation and didn't need to hurry back home. We might never get to the Canary Islands again, so we wanted to stay a few more days. The others dropped us off at a rented apartment in Costa Adeje on their way to the airport.

The Canary Islands are volcanic, so the natural sand is black and rough, not a favorite with beach-loving tourists, so the locals took advantage of nearby natural resources by shipping in white sand from the Sahara Desert. The result is thousands of happy tourists hanging out on the beach and spending money in Costa Adeje.

We spent a couple of hours on the white sand at Playa Torviscos. It was Sunday afternoon, so we wandered through the streets and shops and stumbled on a British sports bar. Singing and laughter poured out of the bar, so we entered to see what was happening. On the big screen television, Andy Murray was playing in the final match at Wimbledon. Peggy had been a college tennis player, so we often watched tennis matches, but seeing Murray become the first British man to win Wimbledon in seventy-seven years while we were sitting in a British sports bar on Tenerife was a classic tennis moment.

Our apartment had a nice balcony, so the next morning Peggy and I ate breakfast on the deck and got in a long conversation about warm islands, beaches, rented apartments with balconies, and our upcoming retirement. We quickly agreed that there was a strong connection between those elements. We hoped these days in Costa Adeje would be a preview to other excursions in the future.

We walked through the shops and restaurants on the boardwalk in the afternoon, and made arrangements for a ferry ride and tour of the island La Gomera the next day. We went to bed that night,

Sammy Sears, left, and Joe Sears climb high above the clouds on Mount Teide (12,198 feet) on Tenerife in the Canary Islands. Teide is the highpoint of Spain and the highest point above sea level in the islands of the Atlantic Ocean. Photo by John Jancik.

A Journey Supporting The Rowell Fund

and I was concerned. Our bus was scheduled to pick us up at seven fifteen, but after the bartering session in Morocco, I had no watch.

No problem. I woke at five a.m. and spent an hour on the balcony writing in my journal before we went to the bus station. On the ferry, we found seats in a bay window, which gave excellent views back to Costa Adeje and ahead to La Gomera.

La Gomera is a different island than Tenerife, smaller but much steeper. Near the coast, it is low grass and bushes, but the road quickly rises to almost 5,000 feet elevation at the dense forest in Garajonay National Park. The slopes are covered with terraces to allow for farming. The deep canyons and volcanic hillsides left earlier farmers with a challenge. Distances across the valleys were too far to yell, but they developed a whistling language which carried the sounds farther and allowed them to communicate greater distances. At our lunch stop, several men and women demonstrated the whistling language, unique to the island of La Gomera, and told us it was a mandatory class at all schools.

La Gomera was the last stop Columbus made before he set sail for the Americas. In San Sebastian, we visited the well where he filled his ships' water supplies and the church where he prayed before he left.

It was also the last spot we visited before we left for America.

Not long after we arrived at home, John contacted me. He remembered an earlier attempt, in 2011, to climb the rock spires on the summit of Echo Peaks in Yosemite National Park. He wanted to give that another attempt. It would not be a 50 for Tibet trip, but just a fun trip in the mountains. We agreed to go there in three weeks, on August 1. It would be a trip that would permanently mark us.

The view of the highest spire on Echo Peaks, Peak #3, from the top of Peak #5.
Photo by John Jancik.

Chapter 13

Yosemite National Park
August 1, 2013

Echo Peaks in Yosemite National Park in California is an imposing mountain. It rises sharply out of the valley and its summit bristles with nine granite spires, which had been numbered rather than named. John and I paused near the base of Echo Peaks. We could see our route ahead of us. The summit spires were brilliant in the early morning sun, and we were excited to get up and play on the peaks.

We cached our extra food, water, and trekking poles under a leaning tree and set out up a gravelly slope in the general direction of a lofty saddle that would take us to the highest of those spires. The morning was chilly, and we were on the west side of the mountain, in the shade. John slipped on his gloves. I had left mine behind. We were climbing in California in August. I didn't expect to need gloves, but now my hands were cold. It was a minor inconvenience. Things could be worse.

The footing on the slope was loose. It was sand and small rock debris, and we slid backwards on almost every step. We worked our way up 300 feet to a series of ledges that would take us to the high saddle. The ledges zig-zagged across the face and gave us a good route up Echo Peaks. We climbed from ledge to ledge, admiring the increasingly beautiful views of Cathedral Peak on the opposite side of the valley. If our morning went well, we planned to climb

Cathedral Peak in the afternoon.

As we neared the saddle between the summit spires, we ran into a section of overhanging rock wall. I moved to our right, scouting a route, but I did not like the looks of it. I suggested to John that we go back to the left and climb up a chute that appeared to lead to the saddle and the spires. John agreed. The chute would take us to the saddle between Peaks 1 and 2, exactly where we wanted to go.

I started up the chute and noticed two rocks the size of shoeboxes covered with many smaller stones. It all seemed loose, and I did not want to knock these rocks off and have them fall down on John. I warned him about the rocks, so he moved to the right, protected by the overhanging wall and out of the way of any rockfall. I carefully moved past the loose rocks. It was easy climbing with rocky blocks on both sides, offering good handholds and footholds. Soon, I was at the top of the forty-foot chute, just below the saddle between the granite spires.

The second I crested that notch, I was in sunshine. After climbing in the shade, I felt warm and welcome. From the saddle, I could see the summits of four peaks, and they were very close. We were on the edge of some really fun and exciting climbing. I could tell that Peak 2 was just a few minutes of scrambling from where I was standing. Peak 3, the highest of the spires, was just behind that. Peak 1 and Peak 2½ were very close. They would be quick climbs for us, once John reached the saddle.

It is generally not safe to have more than one person climb in a chute at a time, so John had remained beneath the rock wall and to the side, out of the line of any falling rocks.

"John, I am on the saddle. It's sunny and warm here. Come on up."

I looked back down the chute and could see John as he worked his way up. Climbers often watch their partners climb for many reasons—safety, to learn more about the rock and techniques, see the motion, help with advice. This time I wish I hadn't watched.

John climbed carefully past the two loose rocks. Above him was a block with a flat top, a natural handhold. John reached up, put his hand on the block, and as he moved up, I heard a clunk, a grinding of the rock and a harsh, throaty shriek from John. Sometimes climbers step up, test a hold, then drop back down to organize their thoughts or take a break. This was clearly not that. John stepped up. The rock gave way, flipping over. John raised his arm over his head as he fell backwards. He and the rock tumbled, disappearing from sight.

"NO! JOHN!" I screamed. The sick feeling, the terror of that moment, haunts me.

The next seconds were a blur, a haze of foggy memory and striking emotion. *This can't be happening*, I thought. *We are always so careful. We take our time. We solve the problems.* This had taken an instant and had gone tragically wrong.

John and I had both been climbing for more than thirty years. Neither one of us had been involved directly in an accident. I suppose it is similar to someone saying he had driven for thirty years and never had a car crash. That can all change in one second.

As I headed back down the chute on Echo Peaks, I was filled with an explosion of fear. My heart was racing. I was breathing in deep gasps. My vision seemed fuzzy, completely out of focus.

John and I had flown into the Reno, Nevada, airport, rented a car, and driven to Mammoth Lakes, California, on July 31, 2013. Forest fires were raging throughout the area and into the edges of Yosemite National Park. Heavy smoke filled the air. Visibility on the highway was poor, and when we passed Lookout Mountain north of Mammoth Lakes, we could see little beyond the edge of the road. We were disappointed. We had talked a long time about climbing Echo Peaks, and we were afraid that the smoke would either stop the climb or take away the views and enjoyment if we did climb.

The next day, August 1, we drove to Yosemite National Park, passing through Lee Vining and driving across Tioga Pass and into Tuolumne Meadows. As soon as we entered the park, the air cleared. We cheered. We parked at the Cathedral Lakes Trailhead and followed the John Muir Trail for twenty minutes, then took the Budd Lake Trail to the wide valley between Echo Peaks and

Cathedral Peak. It took us less than two hours to go from the car to the leaning tree where we cached our water and food.

John said, "We were both excited. It was truly a blue-sky day. Everything was right. Let's go. Let's do this. Let's have fun."

"When I first started falling, it was shocking," John said. "I couldn't believe it was happening."

"I remember Steve reaching the saddle. I was still standing to the right out of sight, but I could hear his voice, and he said it was good to go. I was standing below a large boulder. I looked up, and it did not seem like it would be a difficult move to get up into the notch and then climb up it.

"I had my left hand on a flake of rock and my right foot was about two feet higher than my left foot. I pushed up on my right foot to give me enough elevation to reach up with my right hand. When I put weight on my right hand, the whole boulder moved. I was totally unprepared for that boulder to move. As it moved, I was flung to the side, to my left, out onto the face of the cliff. I fell backwards and down the left side of the chute, and that may have saved my life. I landed on the slope upside down. The large boulder fell past me to my right.

"The one thing I can remember very well is the smell of the rock crashing into the cliff. I will never forget that smell of the rock landing a couple of feet from my right arm. I was falling inverted. I was moving so quickly. On the slope, I was skipping, bouncing down and hitting mostly on my backpack which probably saved me a lot of bruises, scrapes, and scars. The instant after the boulder passed me, I was sledding down the debris we had just climbed up.

"I was out of control. After the rock went by, I was thinking about the cliff below me. I was inverted, so I had no view of where the cliff was. I did not know how close it was, but I thought if I go over that cliff, that will not be a good thing."

"As I was going down the slope, I was upside down and my legs were raised up in the air. I hit a dead tree with my right shin and felt instant pain. It didn't really slow me down too much. I cracked off a branch. Then I hit a green tree with the back of my left knee.

It put a puncture wound right behind my knee. Then I remember hitting a boulder. That slowed me down a lot and spun me around, and I skidded to a stop. I ended up sitting on a ledge facing out. It all happened so quickly."

I have no memory of climbing down the chute. My hands and feet moved instinctively. In what seemed like an instant, I was at John's side. He was sitting on a wide ledge facing away from the mountain. He had clipped a tree branch about two inches in diameter, and it was laying across his legs. I heaved it over the side and looked at him. Nothing seemed out of place, and his face and head looked good. His glasses were still on. I picked up his hat and gave it to him.

His legs were bleeding badly, but I could not tell if they were cuts or abrasions. I asked if he thought anything was broken, and he said he wanted to sit longer before he tried to move.

I looked up and could see where the rock had been, twenty feet above us. The slope down was about forty-five degrees to the spot where we were. There was a two- or three-foot wall just behind John's back. The ledge he was sitting on was about six or seven feet wide. Beyond that was a drop of about three hundred feet down the face we had climbed up on the zig-zag ledges.

"When I was falling, and the boulder was falling beside me, it seemed like that all happened in slow motion," John remembered. "I have heard people that were in accidents talk about that, about things happening in slow motion, and it seemed like that to me. After the boulder passed me, it went from slow motion to whoa, out of control and very fast. My thoughts seemed to race. In a split second, I was thinking about where is the cliff, ouch, I hit a tree. After I hit the first tree limb, until coming to rest, it all happened at light speed."

While John was sitting on the ledge recovering, I thought, *He's got to be able to walk. This is a very bad place to try for a rescue.* I looked down the face to the talus slope and our equipment near the leaning tree. Depending on his condition, it could take us quite awhile to get back down there. It was still early, about nine a.m., but

I did not want to even think about leaving him alone on that exposed ledge and running out to find help.

"I came to a stop and collected myself," John said. "I half expected that something must be broken. How bad are these cuts? I was in pain, shock. What just happened? Things aren't OK. Then I did a sort of random checklist of body parts and pains. What can I move? Do I have any limitations? How bad am I? Then I remember thinking, where did that boulder go? Had it gone over the edge? I remember wondering if I would set off a rock avalanche."

When John felt he could move, he got up. His right knee hurt. He flexed it and said nothing was broken, and he could walk. I was so relieved, and hoped he was right. It was a long ways to our car.

As he was testing his arms and legs, he said the back of his left knee felt bad. He asked if I would look at it. The spot where he had hit the green tree was a cruel gash. It looked deeper than the other cuts, more of a puncture. It was ugly and the cut seemed rougher, more jagged. Blood had run down his calf and pooled at the top of his thick wool sock. I was glad he could not see it. The pain in his right knee seemed to bother him more.

By the time John felt ready to move, the cuts up and down his legs were scabbing. The gloves he had put on at the beginning of the climb were torn and bloody. The gloves had likely saved him a lot of damage to his hands as he skidded down the slope.

Still unsettled from the fall, John wanted to use the rope to descend. I wrapped a sling around the trunk of the tree he hit. I could see the stump of the branch he broke. I set up the rope as a belay to protect him as he downclimbed. With the rope attached to the anchor, I let out just enough rope to allow him to climb down the traversing ledges.

I quickly became concerned because as he moved away from me on the ledge, I realized that, because he was moving horizontally, if he fell with the rope running more sideways than down, he would take a big swing which could be as dangerous as the fall he had already taken. I asked him to stop near a rock flake and bush we had passed on the way up. The ledge was wider there, so he was safe to stand while I removed the anchor from the tree and climbed down to him. Using a smaller tree for the next anchor, I felt better watching him downclimb two or three more of the zig-zag ledges. When he was about fifty feet below me, I had him stop again on a wide ledge. From there, I could move closer to the center of the face and anchor the rope to a larger tree. This was perfect. From that anchor, I could easily watch as John moved slowly back and forth like a long pendulum on the ledges, winding his way down toward the base of the mountain. I was almost directly over the fall line so the belay was a more secure one for him.

He seemed to be moving well, although I knew he was in considerable pain.

"I did not know how stable I was for the downclimb. At times I literally trembled," John said. "I asked if we could rope up. I traversed on the ledges until I reached a place where there was a flat face about six feet high. I remembered climbing up that on the ascent, and I knew it was a short, but tricky move. I did not know if I could make that move. I was intimidated mentally and physically. It wasn't such a hard move, but I had to twist myself around the rock and lower down to the next foothold. In addition to being hurt, I didn't trust myself at all. I couldn't get it out of my head that I had fallen. What had I done wrong?"

Just below the difficult move on the six-foot face, we met three other climbers heading up the route. They stopped to let John climb down the tricky move. When he turned around and walked down to them, they were astounded. John was a mess. For the three guys just seeing him for the first time, he must have looked horrendous. Between the cuts and scraps and the blood that had run down his legs and dried, there was little space on either leg that wasn't bloody.

When John reached the other climbers, he was at the point where the sandy gravel slope touched the granite face of the mountain. He stepped onto the gravel and at that point, no longer needed the rope belay. I untied the anchor from the tree and let the rope slide down the face of the rock. I shouldered my backpack and climbed down to join John and the three other climbers. While I was downclimbing, John explained the accident to them.

By the time I got there, I could tell the group was unsure. John's wounds were not encouraging. That much blood could take the excitement out of anyone's morning enthusiasm. We needed to get John down to the car and eventually to the hospital, so we talked to them briefly, and departed. As we left, two of the climbers said they were done for the day. One set off by himself up the traversing ledges.

John and I walked onto the rocks and sand below. We had cursed the sand on the way up, but now the gentle slide with each step felt good and helped us. We walked back to our cache. There we took a look at his wounds. By then everything was dried solid, including the spot on the back of his left knee. We talked about cleaning off the blood but decided that since everything had dried and sealed, we would leave it. We drank water and Gatorade and ate, then walked across the open valley to meet the trail below Cathedral Peak. We were both relieved to be off the mountain and on the trail, although we knew there would still be some difficult miles ahead.

Chapter 14

ECHO Geophysical Corporation
August 1, 2011

John's fall happened on our second trip to climb on Echo Peaks. Two years earlier, in 2011, we had gone to Bishop to climb White Mountain Peak, at 14,252 feet elevation, the third-highest peak in California. Although high, the climb was an easy walk on an old mining road, but it gave us some beautiful views of the Owens Valley and the tall peaks of the Sierra Mountains. On the way back to town, we stopped at the Ancient Bristlecone Pine Forest to see the twisted and gnarled remains of the bristlecone pine trees, some more than 4,000 years old. They are the oldest trees in the world.

The next day we drove from Bishop to Mammoth Lakes, intending to climb Echo Peaks. John had first become interested in climbing Echo Peaks when "I was looking at a picture book titled *Above Yosemite*. One beautiful panorama shot of the park showed the area near Cathedral Peak and Echo Peaks. It was a land of deep blue sky with spires reaching toward heaven. Yosemite is dramatic and the name Echo is the same as the company I owned. That caught my eye. I looked on the internet to see how difficult these peaks were. I saw that the peaks were exposed Class 3 climbing, and I felt like that was well within my capabilities. They were beautiful rock spires, and I felt like I wanted to climb them."

According to Peter Browning in *Place Names of the Sierra Nevada*, Echo Peak and Echo Creek were probably named by the Wheeler Survey in 1878-79. He noted that the name of Echo Peak was singular until a new map was published in 1922 and the name became Echo Peaks, probably reflecting the multiple granite summits we intended to climb. We had discussed this, and John had suggested that Echo Crest might be a more appropriate name.

On that first trip to Echo Peaks, we left the Cathedral Lakes Trailhead, but became immediately confused. We knew we needed to hike a short distance on the John Muir Trail to find the turn to the Budd Lake Trail which would take us to Echo Peaks. The Budd Lake Trail is used less often than the John Muir Trail and the turnoff is not marked, so we spent some time searching for the turn. We could not find it, so we ended up leaving the John Muir Trail and walking through the forest along Budd Creek for a few minutes, until we encountered the Budd Lake Trail and were back on track.

We hiked that trail to the base of Echo Peaks. We could see several

Scouting out a route on Echo Peaks, Steve Gardiner turned back before a chilly rainstorm kept him and John Jancik trapped in a group of trees for over an hour.
Photo by John Jancik.

of the granite spires on the summit block, and we were excited to get up there and climb them. We selected a route that would take us to a saddle—and we hoped—give us good access to the spires above.

When we reached the saddle, we were surrounded by the spires. We first climbed Peak 5 which gave us breathtaking views of Cathedral Peak, Cockscomb Peak, and others. We knew Peak 3 was the highest, so we scrambled along a ridge toward Peak 1. We would have to climb over Peak 1 to get to Peak 3. The ridge up Peak 1 was very solid granite. It is a dihedral, a corner of two rock faces, like an open book, and we started to climb up it.

"We tried to go across Peak 1 to reach the highest, which is Peak 3," John said. "We started up a dihedral, but decided it was not safe without a rope. I was not comfortable, so we returned and climbed some of the smaller summits."

We climbed three more of the rocky spires, then had the idea that if we descended the route we had climbed up and circled around to the west side of the mountain, we could climb up to the other spires in the area of Peak 3.

Dark clouds were building while we downclimbed the gully. By the time we reached the west side of Echo Peaks, light rain was falling. We huddled under a group of trees and ate lunch. The rain increased, and we sat it out for an hour. By that time, we believed that the rocks would be so wet that the climbing route up Peak 3 would be too dangerous.

We left the tree stand and walked toward Cathedral Peak and the Budd Lake Trail. When we reached the trail, we stopped and gazed up at the route on Cathedral Peak. It is a spectacular peak, the kind that captures a climber's imagination. We had hoped to climb it, too, but the extra time we spent on Echo Peaks and the rainstorm made an attempt on Cathedral Peak a poor choice.

When things go wrong, climbers often say, "Let's leave it for another day." I expect most often, other goals become more interesting and repeating a previous attempt gets forgotten.

It was August 1, 2011. I had a feeling John would want to return.

We were back on August 1, 2013. The date is significant because John and his business partners founded ECHO Geophysical Corporation on August 1, 1986. Our climb in 2011 had been a celebration of ECHO's 25th anniversary. The 2013 return climb was both a chance to finish climbing the remaining spires on Echo Peaks and a celebration of John selling the company on May 31, 2013.

I watched John walk. He seemed to have good balance and moved normally. I knew every step was painful, but he kept moving, and that was what we needed. When we got back on the Budd Lake Trail in 2013, we paused and looked up at Cathedral Peak a second time. We seemed to be cursed regarding that peak. Again, we would not touch it.

John Muir, founder of the Sierra Club and environmental activist who helped preserve Yosemite Valley and many other wildlands, made the first ascent of Cathedral Peak on September 7, 1869. He loved the mountain and the surrounding area. In his book, *The Mountains of California*, he called Cathedral Peak "a temple of marvelous architecture." Muir spent much time in the region around Cathedral Peak. He loved the lakes reflecting the high peaks. He cherished the glaciers. However, even more, he admired the mountains. They inspired him in the same way that European cathedrals moved other people. He called those peaks the "eloquent monuments of the ancient ice-rivers that brought them into relief from the general mass of the range." He said that at first glance, the lakes, rivers, and mountains might seem a jumbled chaos, but if a person looked closely at them, he would eventually see the patterns, the harmony that emerged from the powerful causes of the world to create "Nature's poems carved on tables of stone—the simplest and most emphatic of her glacial compositions."

I let John walk first on the trail, thinking it would be better to let him set the pace. Because the trail often goes over rocky sections, it takes some searching to stay on track. I realized quickly that having him go first meant he was having to keep us on track, as well. Not the right choice. It was too difficult for him to walk and monitor the trail in such pain. I moved in front to do the trail searching and told him to walk at whatever pace was comfortable. I glanced back frequently to keep from getting ahead of him.

We had only been on the trail a few minutes when we met another hiker coming up toward Cathedral Peak. He said hi to me, then his face registered shock when he saw John.

"Can I help you?" he asked. "Do you want me to go back down with you?"

We explained what happened, that we were OK, and would work our way back to the car. Even with everything that had happened to us this day, it was only mid-morning. We would have time to get John off the trail at a reasonable pace and then to the hospital.

In 1986, the oil-and-gas industry hit rock bottom. Prices were low. Companies were laying off employees daily. John and six of his colleagues were among those looking for work. They decided to form a company to give themselves work until the industry recovered. They opened the door of ECHO Geophysical on August 1, 1986.

In the beginning, they hoped to stay in business just long enough for all of them to find work in existing companies. Some of them did. One by one, the co-owners moved on to other ventures. Over the years, the count of original owners dropped from seven to four, then two, and finally one. John became company president in 1999 and sole owner of the company in 2003.

To succeed in an industry that was failing, ECHO had to find a way to stand out, to be unique. John helped the company create a new concept called seismic data pools. Traditionally, companies who needed seismic data would send crews into the field to acquire the reflective seismic data. That data was then their own property. This meant that if several companies wanted seismic data on the same region, they all had to pay to shoot the data. John and his colleagues wanted to create a data pool where several companies could combine their data, making the amount of data much more extensive. Each company could contribute data to the pool and pay an access fee which would allow them to use any data in the pool. The more companies that joined, the more data that would be available.

Such a logical solution to an industry-wide problem made ECHO an immediate success. At first, the seismic data pools were general. Companies could contribute any data into pools with names like SeisMatch and 3D Match. As the concept developed, John believed it would be better to make the data pools area-specific. They took on names like 3D Gulf Coast, 3D Permian Basin, 3D Rocky Mountain, SeisMix California, West Texas SeisTrade, and others. Companies doing oil and gas exploration work always need seismic data, even when the economy is in a low cycle. The data pools gave companies a way to get the data they needed at a reasonable price.

John balanced these data pools with proprietary seismic data processing (processing a company's private data exclusively for them) and revenue sharing (marketing a company's private data for them and splitting the profits). The combination of these three business models kept ECHO going through both the up and down cycles of the oil-and-gas industry. The combination gave them the flexibility to meet client needs.

With that success, ECHO grew, adding more geophysicists, extra marketers, additional office personnel, and eventually growing to a staff of thirty-four. They moved several times into bigger and better office spaces around the downtown Denver area.

For John, however, it wasn't just about selling and processing seismic data. He believed that his company should be strong because of the people who walked in the door every day to work there. He prided himself on hiring the best people he could find, paying them well, and getting out of their way. "Our employees feel empowered," John said," because they are given independence to make decisions on their own. We can do this because of the faith we have in our staff." The focus on quality people was a trademark at ECHO Geophysical Corporation.

One of John's longtime colleagues said, "There is no doubt that people have made ECHO Geophysical successful. The creative idea makers, judicious processors, tireless marketers, conscientious data handlers, and forward-looking financial and administrative advisors have all contributed to ECHO's success. If I were forced to pinpoint one item that contributed above all others to ECHO's long-term success, it would be John Jancik's drive. I've never know anyone with equal determination or passion to make things happen."

Another colleague said, "John is the driving force. He is dynamic, highly motivated, and highly driven. He is always pushing for people to do their best, and because of this, we are able to offer value-priced services that other people in this industry can't offer. John is always in fifth gear. There's not much of an off-switch."

John said, "I expect a lot from my colleagues at ECHO Geophysical, but no more than I expect from myself. I tell everyone on staff that if they are not interested in having the drive in making a positive impact on the company, then they need to find a different place to work. I believe in the concept of hard work potentially providing great opportunities for all employees that care."

John also believed in treating employees fairly. One seismic analyst said, "John is open to new ideas. He trusts us. For example, I work at home one day per week. Because I am not commuting that day, I work longer hours. It is a good situation for both of us."

John is extremely generous. He often spiced up the work week by offering a day off if the Colorado Avalanche won a series in the Stanley Cup Playoffs or if the Denver Broncos made it to the Super Bowl. Hundreds of times his employees, their families, and friends, have attended sporting events and concerts courtesy of free tickets supplied by John Jancik.

John's business model, creative thinking, and employee policies were successful. In fact, they were so successful that by 2013, other, much larger companies wanted ECHO out of the way. One of those companies from Houston wanted to eliminate the competition so badly they made a large cash offer. John hesitated, then finally accepted. He said, "The selling of ECHO Geophysical was definitely a difficult decision to make. I loved many aspects of owning the company, but also realized that after almost twenty-seven years since ECHO's inception, that perhaps it was time to let it go." The Houston company ran a trimmed-down version of ECHO Geophysical Corporation until January 2016, then closed the doors on the company John had built. ECHO Geophysical Corporation was history.

"When we reached our cache at the tree, I opened my backpack, and my camera was in pieces. It was destroyed," John said. "When we got back on the trail, we were moving in spurts, but continuously walking. My legs were stinging. I was concerned about the swelling in my right knee. I thought we should just keep moving. I did not want to stop and let my legs get stiff. I was starting to feel even more pain, because I think the adrenaline was wearing off."

As we walked down the trail, we kept an almost constant stream of conversation going. Part of it was about the physical injuries John had suffered, but more of it focused on the emotional side of the accident. We repeatedly said things like, "How could this be?" "This wasn't supposed to happen. This isn't how it is supposed to go." "We were being so careful. In fact, in the moments up to that fall, we were our most careful, the most careful and preventative that we had been all summer."

They were difficult thoughts, and we were struggling to understand what had happened—and how lucky we had been.

At one point, John said, "You climbed over that rock, and it never moved an inch on you."

He was exactly right. I had climbed up there first. I had moved directly over the rock that had given way for him. Why? Why did it stay when I was there? Did I put my hand at a different angle? Did I have more pressure on my other hand or on a foot? Had I even used the same rock as I moved up? We discussed all those things, and we will probably never know the answers.

Chapter 15

A Matter of Seconds
August 1, 2013

We needed to take a break for lunch. We found a large, fallen tree which would make a good bench. We sat and ate a granola bar and drank water.

John had his backpack at his feet. From a pocket on the back, the face of a stuffed animal, a Wisconsin Badger in a bright red sweater, stared up at me. John grew up in the greater Milwaukee area and was a huge Wisconsin Badgers fan. Alli Bannias bought the fluffy Badger for John, and he had started carrying the little beast on climbing trips as a good luck charm several years before. We had a running joke about "Badgie," as John always called him. John would sneak Badgie into my boots in the tent or leave him peering out of the top of my backpack while I was cooking dinner. He was a spook, stalking me from one mountain venue to the other.

I had no choice, I had to retaliate. I once took photos of Badgie strategically placed under the front tire of our rental car in England. Another time, several stories up, I held Badgie out the hotel window and asked John if Badgie could fly. In a different hotel, John went into the bathroom and found Badgie trapped between the rim and the lid of the toilet.

Badgie had had an interesting life on our climbing trips. As we ate lunch on the log, I realized that in his pocket on the back of John's pack, Badgie was likely the first thing to contact the ground when

John went over backwards and skidded down the mountainside. It may have been minimal, but it was some extra padding.

"I think Badgie took one for the team today," I said.

After our lunch, we resumed walking along the Budd Creek Trail. The trail, in one section, followed closely along the edge of Budd Creek, and we had great views of cascading water splashing on boulders. In some places, the river had cut deep into the bedrock leaving vertical granite walls on both sides. Water tumbled over rocks, dropped over ledges, and sprayed the walls.

Continuing down the trail, I watched John walk. I talked to him. He was doing well, and we were making better progress than I expected. I did not want anything else to go wrong on this trip.

"As we were hiking out to the trailhead, I began recalling the fall more clearly and wondered what, if anything, I did wrong making the pull up move over that large boulder," John said. "However, it would not take long before my thoughts were being interrupted from the pain I felt in both legs, especially my right shin and my right knee." From our cache by the leaning tree to the car was a two-hour walk. Normally that would be time for a recap of the day's climbing and a chat about future goals. On this day, however, the walk had an unearthly feeling to it. We had returned from dozens of climbs together, but we had never had to deal with the emotions and questions we faced after John's fall. It was a difficult walk for both of us.

When John and I reached our rental car at the Cathedral Lakes Trailhead, we put John's jacket on the passenger seat to keep it from getting bloody. He eased himself into the car, and we drove an hour back to Mammoth Lakes. It was a return to the smoky air from the forest fires, but more important for us, it was a trip to the emergency room at the Mammoth Lakes Hospital.

Sitting for an hour in the car made John's legs stiff. He struggled to get out of the car and walk into the hospital.

"Do you need a wheelchair?" the receptionist asked as we entered the front door.

While I parked the car, a nurse escorted John to a bed in the

Suffering multiple cuts, punctures and scrapes during a fall on Echo Peaks in Yosemite National Park, John Jancik displays his bandaged "mummy legs" during a short walk at Lake Tahoe in Nevada.
Photo by Steve Gardiner.

emergency room. When I got back inside, John was on a bed, clearly in pain. The nurse went to get towels and other supplies and asked if I would take John's boots and socks off. His dusty boots came off easily, but the socks, crusted with blood, were much more difficult.

John was worried about his right knee which was causing him serious pain. The nurse wheeled his bed to the X-ray room. Nothing broken, but there must be strained muscles and ligaments.

The nurse used hot, wet towels to soak John's legs. The blood from the cuts and scrapes had gone solid. It took the nurse two hours to get the largest clots to release so he could start working inside the cuts. He cleaned out each cut using a syringe to spray water inside, removing the dirt and gravel. It was a slow process and John seemed to handle it well. It took two more hours to clean the cuts, and near the end, one cut seemed to cause more pain than the others.

"Are you OK?" the nurse asked John.

John said he was lightheaded. The nurse put him on an oxygen machine and that quickly made a difference. I was impressed. With the fall, the walk out, the car drive, and now four hours of intense work in the emergency room, it was the first time John had shown how much it hurt.

When the nurse was ready to clean the deep gouge on the back of John's left knee, I stood and held his leg in the air. For as rough as that one looked, it cleaned up nicely.

With the cuts cleaned, the ER doctor came in and examined the wounds. He was pleased, even complimenting the nurse on how well he had cleaned them. The nurse put ointment on each cut and scrape, then wrapped them in gauze. It took more than a dozen rolls of gauze to cover the cuts and mummy-wrap both legs. His arms, hands, and head were remarkably free from serious injury. Lucky.

The nurse wanted us to return in two days so he could put on a fresh set of bandages and check the wounds for healing. With that, John walked stiff-legged to the car. We picked up a pizza and went to the hotel for the evening.

On the drive south of Lee Vining, John had called Terri to tell her what happened. As a medical doctor, she had a lot of questions for him about his injuries. He assured her that we were on our way to the hospital to get them checked. I knew it was hard for John to call Terri and explain what had happened. I had the same trouble later in the evening when I called Peggy and then Joe Sears to let them know about the accident. John and I were both still incredulous about what had happened, so explaining it to wives and friends was not an easy task.

Our trip to Yosemite was scheduled for four days. With the accident happening on the morning of the first day, we had three more days with no climbing to do. We decided to take a short drive to Obsidian Dome, a lava mound rising some three hundred feet out of the ground. The rocks of the dome are black glass, sharp enough that Paiute Indians used them to make arrowheads. John has degrees in Geology and in Hydrogeology, and loves to talk about geological features as well as rocks and minerals on our trips. His lessons add a lot to each journey, but one time, I decided to tease him. I said something like, "It is fun to climb in Colorado, but I wish we could see some geology. I saw all those mountains and canyons, but there wasn't any geology there. I think geology is just a myth."

On another trip, five of us were driving to a climb and John started talking about geology. "I understand what you are saying, if you believe in that sort of thing," I said. "The myth of geology has really confused a lot of people." As a career English teacher, I added, "What all of that out there really is, is poetry."

Joe Sears, a chemist added, "No, everything out there is really chemistry, not geology." Joe's daughter Sammy, a biology major, said, "Actually, what you are seeing there is biology." My daughter Greta, a musician, stated, "Really, it is all music."

As I walked on the trail around Obsidian Dome with John, I watched his stiff-legged hobble. At that moment, geology seemed all too real. I think I liked it better when geology was a myth.

The next day we went back to the hospital. The nurses changed John's bandages and examined his cuts and bruises. Things were looking as positive as could be expected. He would be in pain for awhile, and there would be scars.

We continued to question what had happened. One question that bothered us: Should we have been roped together before the accident occurred?

This is difficult. While using a rope increases safety, it also slows down the progress of a climb significantly. Because both of us were comfortable with the nature of the climbing we were doing, we hadn't used the rope. Neither of us had felt any reason to tie to the rope that morning on Echo Peaks.

"We talked a lot about if we would ever climb again," John said. "We also talked about why we were not roped in first place. The rock felt safe. Yosemite granite is good. I have thought a lot about this in the time since the accident, and ironically, if I had been roped, I may not have fallen against the cliff to the left. I may have fallen where the boulder went, which could have been fatal. That is a big if, and we will never know for sure, but I have thought about that a lot since that day."

I have had people ask me if I go climbing because of the adrenaline rush. No. I don't like an adrenaline rush. I was recently driving my Jeep on the highway in Montana and hit some ice. The rear end slid to the side. I regained control, but the adrenaline rush from that was strong. Not a good feeling. The good feeling I get from climbing is more like the mindset that psychologist Mihaly Csikszentmihalyi calls flow. Csikszentmihalyi defines flow as the "state in which people are so involved in an activity that nothing else seems to matter; the experience itself is so enjoyable that people will do it even at great cost, for the sheer sake of doing it." It is a state of being absorbed in an activity, of being focused, in the zone.

One of the primary traits of flow state is the balance of challenge and skill. If a task is too difficult, the result is anxiety. If a task is too easy, the result is boredom. This is clear in the sport of mountain climbing and climbers often talk about a peak being too easy to be worth their time or too difficult (at that point in the climber's development) and beyond the climber's ability. The best experiences come when the climb is just beyond the current reach of a climber's talent and he has to stretch a bit, to grow in order to finish the climb well. That is when the climber gains the most from it, learns the most and feels the most satisfaction. This continuous pattern of challenge and growth keeps the climber focused and engaged.

Finding the flow state also comes from having clear goals and accurate feedback, both natural products of climbing. Climbers are notorious for setting lots of goals—for a single climb, for a trip, for a season, for a lifetime. As those goals are attempted, climbers get clear feedback. A missed handhold results in a roped fall and a restart on a rock face. Poor judgment on a weather condition means getting soaked in an afternoon thundershower. Choosing the best route leads a climber easily to the summit and back down safely. Humans want to understand how their actions affect their goals and clear feedback, like that provided in climbing, is excellent motivation for wanting to learn more. For example, in teaching, I often work with a student for weeks or months and sometimes cannot tell if my work actually made a difference for that student. Sometimes it is very clear, but sometimes it is not. Yes, I may get a letter years later telling me that I made a difference, but it might not always be clear to me, and it might not give me the feedback I need in a timely manner. Climbing is more clear-cut on this. You make the summit or you don't. You reach the top of the cliff or you don't. Those exact responses are a powerful part of the climbing experience.

Flow activities also result in a transformation of time. Being engaged in an activity fully means there is little mental space left to think about anything else. If a person is asking the question, "Am I in flow?" the answer is no. When a person is involved in an optimal experience, time is suspended.

In addition, there is a related state called social flow, which happens when sharing important events with significant people. Team sports fit well in this area, and climbing offers a scenario where participants must trust each other to a high degree. Mountain climbing suits this, and all other aspects of flow, well.

The adrenaline from my Jeep sliding or from watching John fall are ugly feelings, caused by fear and a sense of being out of control. The flow that comes from dreaming about a good climb, planning the logistics and travel, then executing the plan on the mountain is highly motivational, deeply rewarding. Those actions lead to the life-changing, positive results of mountain climbing.

Not every mountain climber feels this way. Reinhold Messner, the first person to climb Mount Everest without bottled oxygen, to solo-climb Everest, and to climb all fourteen of the 8,000-meter peaks, felt driven to push closer and closer to the edge of death while climbing. In his book *My Life at the Limit*, Messner said, "It is through resisting death that we humans experience what it is to be human. And it is in this seeming paradox that the most fundamental reasons for climbing mountains or seeking out extreme situations are to be found, whether it's the South Pole, the North Pole, the Gobi, K2, or Chang Tang. The secret lies in the fact that I can only have the most intense experiences when I push myself to the limits of what is possible. Obviously, when I'm doing that, I hope that I won't die and that nothing bad will happen to my partner, that everything will go well. I also know that if I just go for a bit of a hike, the experience will not be so intense."

It is that attitude that made Messner the greatest high-altitude mountaineer that has ever lived. His desire to confront death in the mountains and feel the success of overcoming a desperate situation is a different level of motivation. He continued, "It is this experience—not dying itself—that you want to have again. I keep hoping to experience it again but without anything bad happening. It's got nothing to do with having a death wish; it's all about hungering after the experience. I'm not caught between the fear of death and a death wish, but between the feeling of terror that I might die when I'm up there and the joy of having survived."

My motivation is different. It is more aligned with flow and seeking to become engaged in a climb, to enjoy a day with friends, to see beautiful scenery, and savor a mountain experience. Messner's drive to push the limits worked for him. His exploits on the hardest mountains in the world are legendary. But that is not my world of mountain climbing.

Motivation for John is based on "being drawn to the top of a mountain through a journey of many steps. There are many details that go into a successful climb and I love each aspect of them. It is like putting a jigsaw puzzle together. The experience of reaching a summit can provide memories that last a lifetime."

John and I had gone to Echo Peaks hoping for a sunny day and the chance to climb several of the spires. However, during the day, we experienced a bit of the terror Messner talked about.

That evening, in our hotel room, I noted in my journal: *I don't know if I want to climb again. I hate the thought that this happened, and I wish somehow we could change it, but I will be forever grateful that it was no worse. Given the location and potential, we came out of it well. I have had so many good years of climbing, perhaps it is time to reflect on the wonders I have seen and experienced and find new activities for my time and energy. I do not want to see another accident.*

When the nurses at the hospital changed John's bandages, they gave him a choice of color. He picked neon green. When we went to the Reno airport to fly home, he wore a pair of shorts. Everyone in the airport stared at him. They should have.

It was hard to say goodbye at the airport. It had been a difficult few days with the accident and the disappointment of being so close to so many excellent climbs, yet not completing any. It was an emotional time.

We talked daily after we both returned home. John had to wear the bandages a few weeks. One day he emailed me: *My legs are still fairly heavily bandaged. The cuts and scrapes behind my right thigh are just not healing. Also that puncture wound on my right shin is slow to completely scab over. The knee still hurts from the sprain, and it is still slightly swollen. It is on the mend, though. I still look back at what happened and cannot believe it. I am more frustrated than anything at this point, because we had such a good day going for us, and everything looked like a go for both Echo Peaks and Cathedral Peak. Our route finding was impeccable, and the safety level that we were climbing at was not even in question. To have something go wrong so fast and so close to being a major disaster was indeed scary, and continues to be. The lingering emotional wounds will take a lot longer to heal than the actual wounds I am enduring. Perhaps the mountain just 'wins' sometimes.*

After John's legs healed, John and I, along with his brother-in-law Paul Konichek and nephew Aaron Konichek, went into the San Juan Mountains in southwestern Colorado to climb an absolutely beautiful mountain called Wetterhorn Peak. John had climbed the 14,016-foot peak several years before and wanted the rest of us to see it. The first few hours of hiking are on a good trail that winds its way up onto a ridge leading to the summit block. The last five hundred vertical feet are steep and exposed.

We were having an enjoyable day in the mountains until we got to the steep section. At that point, John said, "By the time we were near the base of the Prow on the ridge, we had crossed several steep gullies filled with dirt and rock. Each step I took, I questioned the handholds and my footing. The climb was becoming a mental task more than a physical one. Finally, after climbing up one steep gully, I realized that I was not enjoying the moment at hand but actually fearing it. I stopped and called out for Steve. I had never turned around below the summit on a Colorado 14er, but that day would be the first time. My mind raced back to the Yosemite fall repeatedly. Everything looked so good on that climb, and it almost all went wrong. I wondered if history could repeat itself for me. I was upset at myself. This was not the way I wanted the day to go."

I walked down with John to a flat, grassy area where he would be comfortable, then climbed back up. The rest of us climbed to the summit of Wetterhorn Peak, spent a few minutes enjoying the view, then climbed down to John. I knew he was disappointed. He had wanted to convince himself he was past his concern for exposure, but he hadn't received that confirmation.

"Ever since the uncomfortable situation on the Wetterhorn," John said, "I have had the feeling of being lost in terms of climbing. I really do not want to give up mountaineering, but are my days over where I take on questionable exposure? I just don't know. In one sense, I feel like I have had enough fun in my life that it makes little sense to keep pushing the odds. But, on the other hand,

I cannot imagine my hopes to climb mountains like Echo Peaks and Cathedral Peak being over. It is amazing how life can change in just a matter of seconds."

Stinging physically, mentally, and emotionally from the fall in Yosemite, John decided he wanted another adventure trip, but a more relaxed one. Five months later, in January 2014, he gathered eight family members and headed to Australia to climb Mount Kosciuszko, an opportunity for them to stand on the highpoint of a country and continent at the same time. It is one of the famed Seven Summits, the highest peak on each of the seven continents.

The group flew to Sydney, where they spent three days recovering from the long flight and fourteen-hour time change. After sightseeing in Sydney, they flew to Canberra and drove to the trailhead on January 5.

Mount Kosciuszko in Australia gives climbers the chance to reach the highpoint of both a country and a continent at the same time. Standing on its summit are David Baker, Alizah Baker Morse, Jacob Artz, Dan Giles, Sebastian Eyre, Jessica Morse, and John Jancik. Seated are Astrid Eyre and Ashley Baker.
Photo courtesy of John Jancik.

Mount Kosciuszko, at 7,310 feet above sea level, is located in Kosciuszko National Park in New South Wales on the east coast of Australia.

John explained, "The climb was a straightforward hike from Charlotte's Pass which is about at timberline. An established trail runs five-point-six miles to the summit of Mount Kosciuszko. For the first two-thirds of the climb, you never see the peak but get wonderful views of Australia's high alpine environment. Along the way, you cross the headwaters of the famous Snowy River."

Summit day was mostly clear with wind gusts up to forty mph, making the temperature on top about twenty degrees with wind chill. The team of nine split into two groups, with John leading one up the Charlotte's Pass route. With John were Jacob Artz, Jessica Morse, and Dan Giles. David Baker led another group up the Thredbo Route, a four-point-one-mile trail that joins the Charlotte's Pass Route just below the summit. With David were Ashley Baker, Alizah Baker Morse, Sebastian Eyre, and Astrid Eyre. All nine reached the summit.

John said, "Australia is a wonderful country and virtually everyone we met along the way was very engaging with us and nice to talk with. The scenery varied tremendously for us as we visited the metropolitan city of Sydney, the mountain town of Thredbo, and the Great Barrier Reef. We had a taste of three unique places."

After the climb, the group spent six days on Hayman Island in the Whitsunday Island group of the Great Barrier Reef, snorkeling, diving, sea kayaking and paddle-boarding in the tropical paradise.

"The Yosemite wounds seemed etched into me physically and emotionally," John said, "but highpointing Australia was a good first step back towards hiking and climbing again. However, I knew I still had a long way to go before I was confident of taking on harder objectives." With the trip to Australia behind him, John turned his interests toward the Maritime Provinces of eastern Canada.

Chapter 16

The Top of the Maritime Provinces
July 4, 2014

With John in Denver and me in Billings, we did not see each other for many months after the Yosemite trip. We did talk almost daily, on the phone or by email, and I listened as he described the healing of his many cuts and bruises. He told me about the pains and the eventual scars. The experiences of John's fall had shaken us both, in different ways, but deeply. It was hard for both of us to question our love of the mountains, our desire for adventures. We wondered if we would, or should continue with our trips, and if we did, what would those trips look like.

One day, John sent a photo of Mount Carleton, the highpoint of New Brunswick, a province in eastern Canada. It is a beautiful peak and a straightforward hike on a trail. No exposure. No chance for a fall like we experienced in Yosemite. Maybe something like that would be a good place to start as we reevaluated our priorities and dreams. We did some research and added Nova Scotia and Prince Edward Island to our trip that became the Top of the Maritime Provinces.

Arriving from various locations, our group of five met at Denver International Airport. In addition to John, our team included Joe Sears and his daughter Sammy (who had been with us in Africa and Iberia), my daughter Greta (who had joined us on Mount Shasta), and me.

At the airport, I found Greta first. As we walked to meet the others, I was nervous. I hadn't seen John in months and although he said his wounds had healed and his pain was gone, I hadn't seen the results myself. When we saw him standing near our departure gate, we shook hands, and then he showed us his scars. The story of his fall was written on his legs.

It was good for all of us to be together again. It was good to be launching a new trip, but there was a sense of caution in the air. Had the fall changed us? Would we still be the same adventurous group, laughing and talking about past events, dreaming about future ones?

One other thing was different. In the past, we had canceled, rerouted, hurried, or otherwise changed trip plans to accommodate work obligations, family concerns, travel connections, sickness, injuries, rain, snow, heat, cold, and other variables. We had never altered itineraries because of a hurricane, but Hurricane Arthur was nearing Florida and the forecast was for it to follow the East Coast as far north as Nova Scotia, an unusual event. When we planned the trip, we did not include hurricane options.

From Halifax, we drove north and east across the eight-mile-long Confederation Bridge onto Prince Edward Island. Residents of the island have mastered the art of carving out just enough trees to place a home and outbuildings precisely in a frame of forest. We admired their planning and work as we drove through the countryside. The appropriately nicknamed "Gentle Island" is nearly flat, with some low hills rising. The unnamed highpoint of Prince Edward Island is only four hundred and sixty-six feet in elevation and is hidden in some trees on the edge of a potato field. It is not visited often, so the trail into the trees was overgrown, but with the help of a GPS unit, we were able to follow the trail several hundred yards into the trees and locate the post and mailbox that mark the provincial highpoint. It is another example for us of a highpoint that is not an interesting climb or a challenging peak, but without the search for this obscure location in the trees, we would not have enjoyed the absolute beauty that is Prince Edward Island.

The next day we drove back across the Confederation Bridge and turned north through New Brunswick to Bathhurst. Throughout the day, weather reports sounded terrible. Our climbs in New Brunswick and Nova Scotia were imperiled. If the hurricane kept on track, even driving or being in the area might be a problem. Light rain provided a preview of what the reports said would be heavy rain for the next several days. After a short walk through downtown Bathhurst, we ended up back at our hotel, sitting in chairs in the lobby, involved in what became a long series of stories about many of the adventures we had shared together. We told stories of Alaska, Quetico, Greenland, and Kilimanjaro. We revisited Rainier, Granite Peak, Katahdin and Shasta. We relived the rime ice on Iliniza Norte and the rock storm on Chimborazo. We laughed. We remembered. We shared our fears over Romney's problems in Africa. We recounted the horror of John's fall in Yosemite.

We talked for an hour. Then another. The rain hit the windows of the lobby and splashed in the parking lot in front, but we continued talking. These were the stories of our lives. They were the bonds of our collective friendships. Yes, we all had our separate careers, our professional lives, and were doing well with those, but within this group, the adventures and the dreams they manifested were our passion. For Joe, John, and me, these adventures were an important aspect of each of our lives, and as the years had passed and our children had grown, we had been able to share the adventures with them, as well.

The morning of July 4 looked bleak. The sky was dark. Heavy clouds threatened. We were a two-hour drive from Mount Carleton, so we had no choice but to set out and hope we would get a break. It had been a photo of Mount Carleton that had inspired John to suggest the Maritime Provinces trip. Mount Carleton (2,680 feet) was the highest of the peaks we scheduled for this trip, so it became a sort of focal point in our plans. The dark skies gave us little hope, but the steady rain from the day before had eased off to an occasional mist.

We arrived at Mount Carleton Provincial Park, and the clouds seemed to rise slightly, a beckoning to us to leave the car and hike.

"The night before, we didn't give ourselves much of a chance of climbing Mount Carleton," Joe said. "By the time we got to the trailhead, it looked like we would have a chance, and we were anxious to leave the car and walk because of the thick clouds of mosquitos that were swarming around us. I don't know if I have ever seen them that thick."

The trail was three miles through dense forest. That, with the dark clouds, made the full day feel like dusk. Just before the top, we broke out of the forest and scrambled on rocky slopes to the summit. We had visibility to nearby peaks, but nothing in the distance. We ate lunch near the iconic wooden hut built on the summit and took our photographs.

We had expected the worst. We had our raincoats, gloves, stocking caps and boots, ready to walk in rain and mud, but we had been lucky. Our descent was dry.

The heavy rain waited until the next day. As we drove south from Bathhurst to Nova Scotia, the highway was a river. Joe drove slowly, keeping the car solid on the road. The windshield wipers flapped all day. We read. We listened to more reports that the hurricane winds and rain had reached southern Nova Scotia.

"I felt like the car was on the edge of hydroplaning half the time," Joe said. "The whole idea of trying to go climbing in the middle of a hurricane in Canada seemed so bizarre."

We made it as far as Truro and stopped there. We had read about the bore tide that roared up the channel at Truro and decided we wanted to see this unique phenomenon. We went out to the point where we should see it, and waited in staggering wind for an hour. No bore tide. The wind had flattened it. We did take some time to drive up nearby Nuttby Mountain, the highpoint of mainland Nova Scotia. The winds from the dying hurricane made standing on top of Nuttby Mountain a chilly challenge.

We drove east across the Canso Causeway to Cape Breton Island and the town of Ingonish. White Hill, the highpoint of Cape Breton Island and the province of Nova Scotia, rises slightly above the rest of Cape Breton Highlands National Park, so a permit is required to hike there. The remote nature of this highpoint and the long

A Journey Supporting The Rowell Fund

approaches from any direction make it an unpopular destination, so our questions in the park office drew an audience. We got our permit and a map, then went to Ingonish Beach and waded in the freezing waters that surround Cape Breton Island.

We had found driving directions from Ingonish to Cheticamp (SHET-ee-camp) Lake, about an hour and a half of travel on winding, dirt roads with no signs or indicators of distance or direction. We managed to find the parking area, but were immediately confronted with a serious problem. The route around Cheticamp Lake goes along the eastern shore, but a man-made drainage ditch from Cheticamp Lake blocks the path a few steps from the car. I went downstream, assuming that it would widen and be shallow enough to cross, but the hurricane rains of the previous days were again causing us problems. The runoff was much too deep and swift to cross safely.

There is a flow control station near the parking area, but a chain-link fence on each side discouraged us from crossing it. After exhausting all other options, however, we hoisted backpacks over the fences and crawled across.

The walk around Cheticamp Lake was a mixture of gravel, mud, piles of driftwood, and stream crossings. We had the map from the Park Office with us and located the spot, near a small stream, where an old ATV trail reached the north shore of Cheticamp Lake. Near the stream, the grass and bushes were low and easy to walk, but twenty or thirty yards to the east, the thick bushes formed a green wall, so spotting any sort of trail entrance was difficult. We spread ourselves along the stream and approached the wall of bushes and low trees, hoping one of us would see something helpful. I went farthest left and entered a group of trees. I couldn't see anything that looked like a trail, but I did find a discarded moose antler. It had been lying there long enough that it was partially covered in mud. I pried it from the ground and picked it up. It weighed nearly forty pounds, and I carried it out to the area where the others were searching. Just as I reached the opening and could see the others, I heard Joe yell that he had found a rock cairn that might be the marker for the elusive trail.

We took a few photos of and with the moose antler, then propped it against a tree. Joe led us to what can only be called the pathetic remains of a rock cairn. We looked into the trees. Perhaps it was a maintained trail at one time, but it had long since outgrown any trimming that might have been done. It required a lot of engineering to negotiate that trail, especially the first two hundred yards up a hill. After that, it opened somewhat so we could move easier, although the soaking rains left their mark with deep puddles and extensive mud. We moved forward in low gear.

The landscape of the highlands is almost featureless. Every small hill looks the same. Low trees and bushes extend in every direction. Dense clouds above added to the flatness of the scene. Somewhere in front of us, one of those hills was just enough higher than the rest to have been measured the highpoint. That distinction would have been mechanical. No human eye could ever see a difference.

We followed the ATV trail for two-point-six miles. We had a

Heavy rains and high winds from Hurricane Arthur had battered Cape Breton Island in Nova Scotia for days before John Jancik (left), Sammy Sears, and Joe Sears hiked through mud, gravel, and piles of driftwood along the shore of Cheticamp Lake in an attempt to reach White Hill in the Cape Breton Highlands.
Photo by Steve Gardiner.

GPS waypoint marked where we planned to leave the ATV trail and bushwhack toward White Hill. It sounded like a good plan, but the trail never reached the waypoint. The ATV trail dwindled into nothingness half a mile from where we expected to begin bushwhacking. We faced a thick stand of alders, unsure of where we could go.

We tried several excursions into the alders. Scratches covered our arms and legs. Deep streams we could not cross blocked our way. We retreated and tried again. And again. It was clear that we were not going to breach the alder stand, so we returned along the ATV trail to a spot that looked more approachable. The GPS showed that we were just under a mile from the summit of White Hill. We were unsure which spot we were heading for, and these attempts were disorienting in a landscape with no distinguishing features and gray, heavy skies, but we set out into the alders once again.

It was painfully slow. In fact, at one point, I checked my watch and then the GPS. We had covered one-tenth of a mile in twenty minutes. It had taken us four-point-five hours to get this far, so that meant the same time to get out. With the summit still nine-tenths of a mile away through more bands of trees and alders, it was clear we could not reach the highpoint and get out by dark. The trail was hard enough to follow in the day—we did not want to try it at night. Compared to the trip reports we had read, our trip conditions were highly affected by the hurricane. We slogged through miles of mud. The streams were impassable. The bushwhacking was too thick, too endless. It was an interesting and unique hike, but our chance had passed.

We ate lunch and retraced our path on the ATV trail to the stream at Cheticamp Lake. We walked past the moose antler we had left propped against the tree in the morning and stopped at the inlet. While getting a drink, we watched a moose come to the shore. When he saw us, he ran a short distance, then stopped to look at us again. It must be a rare sight to see human beings in that place.

The waves chopped high on Cheticamp Lake and the wind blew in our faces as we circled back, arriving at our car more than nine hours after leaving it.

If there is a physical symbol of the adventures we have shared as part of the 50 for Tibet project, it is the American flag we unfurled on summits and at significant locations. We have thousands of photos of us holding the same flag, various combinations of smiling people surrounding us. To look at the flag, it doesn't seem anything special. It is a medium-sized Stars and Stripes that John bought in Littleton, Colorado. A humble beginning, but its stature changed quickly.

John bought it for the 1996 American Top of the World Expedition, hoping to take it to the summit of Star Spangled Banner Peak, which we did, but the first time we unfurled it was on Top of the World Island in the Arctic Ocean off the northern coast of Greenland. We held the flag aloft, celebrating our victory in the high Arctic. We took photos of ourselves, the islands, and the flag. It was the first of many such moments.

In our two Greenland expeditions, the flag went to the top of fifteen peaks. It has been to three continental highpoints. It went with us to Kilimanjaro, the Top of Africa, in 2002. I took it to Aconcagua, the Top of South America, in 2005. John took it to Kosciuszko, the Top of Australia, in 2014. It has been to the top of seventeen peaks over 14,000 feet elevation in Colorado. When John proposed the 50 for Tibet project, the flag was recruited to the team. It accompanied varying combinations of John and his friends to forty-eight state highpoints.

In 2010, John and I took the flag to the British Isles and the highpoints of Scotland, England, Wales, Ireland, and Northern Ireland. In 2011, the flag went to Scandinavia to visit the highpoints of Denmark, Sweden, Finland, and Norway. It has been to the top of Mount Fuji, the highpoint of Japan. It spent time on the highest peaks in Spain and Portugal as well as the Rock of Gibraltar.

In addition to highpoints, the flag has traveled to other unusual locations. It visited the North American continental lowpoint in Death Valley, California, the geographical center of the U.S. in South Dakota, and three geographic boundary tri-points, including Kansas-Missouri-Arkansas, Colorado-Nebraska-Wyoming, and Norway-Sweden-Finland. Although not highpoints, two other challenging peaks are on the flag's resume—Mount Shasta in California and Iliniza Norte in Ecuador.

"One of my favorite memories of the flag was holding it on the summit of Helvetia Tinde, the highest peak in the northernmost mountain range on Earth," John said. "Making the first American ascent and the second ever ascent, we held it up on the summit along with the exact British flag that had been there twenty-seven years earlier on the mountain's first-ever ascent."

If that flag could talk, the stories it could tell.

In 2006, John created the concept of 50 for Tibet. It was a chance to travel, to hike and climb, to share adventures with friends, and to honor the memory of Galen and Barbara Rowell by helping The Rowell Fund for Tibet support Tibetan writers, artists, and musicians. He hoped to climb all 50 state highpoints in one year. Life intervened, and the project stretched into a second year, then a third year. Then the highpointing concept expanded to international destinations. Now, more than a decade after its start, 50 for Tibet has not met its initial goal, but added so much more to the lives of its participants and to the mission of The Rowell Fund for Tibet. New ideas have kept the project alive and strong, and though we may not know where 50 for Tibet will take us in the future, we know for sure that the team's motto of "Celebrating One Mountain Culture to Preserve Another" will continue to be a good guide to our adventures.

John said, "It just is not enough to be a spectator in today's world. We must be active, involved and passionate about helping others whether it be the homeless shelter in your hometown or Tibetans halfway around the world. Living life is what it is all about."

At his home in Dharamsala, India, the Dalai Lama meets with Tencho Gyatso, Lizzy Ludwig, John Jancik, Terri Baker, Jacob Artz, Jessica Morse, and Dan Giles.
Photo courtesy of John Jancik.

Epilogue
by John Jancik

The domestic and international highpoints. The fundraising for The Rowell Fund For Tibet. The Tibetan people around the world. Galen and Barbara Rowell.

They were all part of 50 For Tibet. Perhaps the adventure was about them all. Perhaps the goal was the journey and not the destination. No matter how defined, 50 For Tibet accomplished a lot during its passage of time. Perhaps the numbers actually say it all.

A total of **67** highpoints.

Over **$250,000** raised by 50 For Tibet and Terri and I

The **7,000,000** plus Tibetans around the world.

Two extraordinary, wonderful individuals.

As the United Airlines 747 jet touched down in New Delhi, India, in September 2014, I was not just jetlagged from my flight from the United States, I was full of anticipation and wonder. I had never been to India before, and this trip I already knew would be special.

Included in the group I was traveling with were Terri and her oldest daughter, and occasional highpoint participant, Jessica. Also in the party were Lizzy Ludwig, Deputy Director of Development for the International Campaign For Tibet (ICT), and Tencho Gyatso, the Director of Tibetan Empowerment & Chinese Engagement Programs for ICT. Born in Dharamsala, India, the seat of His Holiness the Dalai Lama and the exile Tibetan administration, Tencho moved to the United States in 1999 after serving as an elected member of the

Tibetan Parliament-in-exile for two terms. Tencho, the niece of the Dalai Lama, is one of the kindest and most enthusiastic people I have ever met.

The group, which initially spent a couple days exploring New Delhi, eventually traveled by plane to Dharamsala in northern India. Dharamsala is a city in the upper reaches of the Kangra Valley and is surrounded by a dense coniferous forest consisting mainly of beautiful Deodar cedar trees. Located in the shadow of the Dhauladhar mountains., Dharamsala is the center of the Tibetan exile world in India.

In May 1960, the Central Tibetan Administration (CTA) was moved to Dharamsala after previously fleeing Tibet. His Holiness the 14th Dalai Lama soon established residence as well there. Since then, Dharamsala has become the center of Tibetans in exile in India.

On disembarking the plane at the the Dharamsala Gaggal Airport, we were met by Kalden Tsomo from the CTA. Kalden became the group's constant companion for the rest of our time in Dharamsala. She was gracious in helping our group learn about the Tibetan culture.

During our week in Dharamsala, our group was privileged to meet with many recipients of grants from The Rowell Fund For Tibet. Tencho had arranged for these gatherings so that we would have first-hand observation of the impact that the fund was making on important and key projects. Perhaps my favorite moment was when Terri and I were able to give a slide show of 50 For Tibet for the staff and students of the Tibetan Children's Village (TCV) school. While I went through the photographs shown on a very large screen in an auditorium, I was very excited about the fact that the 50 for Tibet adventure had now reached Tibetan children on the other side of the world from Colorado. A truly memorable experience.

Perhaps the ultimate highlight and certainly the greatest honor was our group's opportunity to meet with the Dalai Lama at his residential complex. It is hard to describe the feeling when he warmly shakes your hand, looks directly into your eyes and places the blessed Khata scarf around your neck. For Terri, whom the Dalai

A Journey Supporting The Rowell Fund 177

Lama leaned over and pressed his forehead against hers, it was very special, as well.

The meeting was one of indescribable joy, spiritual awakening and of tremendous respect for this Nobel Peace Prize winner. To say it was a life-altering time would not be an overstatement. Jessica added, "Meeting the Dalai Lama feels like a dream. He is a person I admire and respect, and it was definitely an honor to be in his presence and listen to his perspective. After meeting him and seeing the reactions of others, honestly, I felt undeserving of the opportunity."

Reflecting back on our time in Dharamsala, Tencho stated, "It was a such a pleasure showing you and Terri around Dharamsala, and introducing you to the many projects and people that the Rowell Fund has supported over the years. Special for me, in particular, was the audience with His Holiness, the conversation session with the newly arrived youth from Tibet at Sherab Gatsel Ling Transit school and the visit to the Tibetan Children's Village school where we met the young kids from the photography club sponsored by a Rowell grant. It was wonderful to see you hit it off immediately with the kids from the photography club and what a lovely surprise for all, when you decided to separate with your DSLR camera and gift it to them. I remember the expression on your face and the expression on the young teacher who runs the club ... captured in two words - pure happiness."

Lizzy also commented, "I have so many incredible memories. Of course, walking the kora around the Tsuklakhang and reflecting on our audience with His Holiness, during which His Holiness stressed the importance of the work of The Rowell Fund and encouraged further efforts, was unforgettable. But there were so many other memorable experiences- visiting the Library of Tibetan Works & Archives and watching as the Director showed you and Terri the inscription thanking The Rowell Fund for funding one of their publications, observing the Tibetan Parliament in session, during which The Rowell Fund and our delegation were so kindly mentioned and welcomed, meeting the students of the Photography Club at the Tibetan Children's Village School, not to mention the hospitality, countless cups of tea, khatas, warm words and smiles with which we were greeted at each of our meetings. But I think one of the most memorable moments for me was on our last morning in Dharamsala when we had breakfast with the teacher who lead the Photography Club at TCV and you and Terri so generously donated your beautiful camera and projector to add to the Club's equipment. It was such a joyous moment for everyone involved, and one that really encapsulated the spirit and impact of The Rowell Fund. It's a moment, among a treasure trove of wonderful memories, that has especially stuck with me."

To say that Tencho and Lizzy were instrumental in the planning and organizational part of the trip is a vast understatement of their role and companionship in our trip to India. The smile on their faces greeted us every day and made the visit one of happiness and joy. Tencho commented, "Your commitment and dedication to helping Tibetans over these many years is inspiring to everyone on the Rowell Board and all of us at ICT. So, I felt honored and grateful that I could bring you both to visit many of the (Rowell Fund For Tibet) grantees. It was a special pleasure for me to be your travel partner on this first trip to visit with the Tibetan grantees and experience the community whom you both supported with so much heart over these many years."

Jessica also commented about the trip: "Honestly, all of the highpoints and fundraising over the years hadn't made much sense to me until I met with the grantees and other Tibetans in Dharamsala. In fact, I didn't know much about their current status or their history. This is when everything sunk in, and I realized why you do what you do, and why The Rowell Fund and International Campaign for Tibet is so important. I loved how grateful and excited everyone was to receive funds that supported a cause they were so passionate about and kept their culture alive. I feel privileged that the Tibetans had welcomed us into their culture and shared so much information. I hope to never forget some of the most unbelievable moments such as the Children's Village, the Library Archives, the Tibetan Medical Institute, the political meeting, the trade school, and of course, the speeches from the Dalia Lama."

A Journey Supporting The Rowell Fund

Returning home from Dharamsala, India, I reflected on being able to finish the circle of 50 For Tibet's fundraising mission for The Rowell Fund. I was more proud than ever of what we all accomplished. Team HighPoint's passion to succeed was unwavering and steadfast. No highpoint was insignificant, and no dollar raised for The Rowell Fund was too small.

John Ackerly added, "The 50 for Tibet project really got The Rowell Fund into high gear and kept it there for years. Without 50 for Tibet, The Rowell Fund would have hobbled along, with not even half the funds for projects that it ended up having. 50 for Tibet also brought lots of publicity to the overall Tibetan cause, and brought excitement within the Tibet movement."

John Mitchler also offered, "As Editor of the Highpointers Club quarterly magazine, I have watched the development of the 50 for Tibet initiative, and was always eager to publish updates and promote what I believe is one of the most significant cultural causes in the world. Visiting the 50 highpoints has become an attractive vehicle for many charities lately, but none have pursued it with the conviction and success seen by 50 for Tibet. The expansion of their mission to country highpoints around the world has definitely added a unique angle to their story, and proves their deep support for Tibet."

It was ultimately really never about the highpoints after all. It was about the journey for over ten years of travel, fund raising and raising awareness of the Tibetan cause. Along the ways, many highpoints, mountains, hills and simple landscape "bumps" were climbed. David Baker reflected, "I'm happy with what I did. I was never a peak bagger, but I do enjoy summiting. Getting all fifty highpoints for me was never a primary goal as much as trying to raise awareness for The Rowell Fund For Tibet was. Beyond that, I am thrilled that I got the opportunity to spend so much time traveling around the U.S. with friends. It was an experience that not many get to live, and I'll always be grateful for that."

For me, a dream of visiting state highpoints had turned into something a whole lot larger. A journey undertaken with only trying to reach those highpoints in the beginning had evolved into reaching a place where my very being had now been fundamentally altered. Yes, mountains such as Kebnekaise, Mount Rainier, Granite Peak, Mount Pico, Katahdin, Mount Whitney, Ben Nevis and Mount Fuji were tremendous, exciting experiences. And there is no doubt that I love mountaineering. Even when struggling through a major storm on Ecuador's Chimborazo, I enjoyed and appreciated the place and the moment I was at. Maybe it was a lesson in humility and respect? Maybe something else? But one thing I did come to know was that climbing and highpointing for a cause was what my destiny was meant to be.

I have been truly blessed with family and friends who have supported me through this journey around the world. Furthermore, The Rowell Fund For Tibet, which is a vehicle to enrich, preserve and celebrate Tibetans no matter where they live, is something that has taken me to places and people whom I never would have known otherwise. Who could have realistically asked for anything better? It is a privilege to give back to others.

The world as we know it now includes but also excludes—in some ways—Tibet. However, Tibet is more than a high altitude landscape with borders. It is a people, a way of life, a sense of spirit and a measuring stick as to the preservation of a culture that is trying to survive. I do not know if it will. But I can try. We all can try. And if we don't, we will lose some of ourselves as well.

> "We are visitors on this planet. We are here for ninety or one hundred years at the very most. During that period, we must try to do something good, something useful, with our lives. Try to be at peace with yourself, and help others share that peace. If you contribute to other people's happiness, you will find the true goal, the true meaning of life."
> **--- His Holiness the 14th Dalai Lama**

A Journey Supporting The Rowell Fund 181

Ice flows over the rocks below The Castle on Chimborazo.
Photo by Steve Gardiner.

Dawn clouds near the summit of Mount Fuji in Japan.
Photo by John Jancik.

About Steve Gardiner

Steve Gardiner taught high school English and journalism for 38 years in Wyoming, Montana, and Peru. He is a National Board Certified Teacher and the 2008 Montana Teacher of the Year. He holds a Doctorate of Education degree. He has published articles in *The New York Times, The Chicago Tribune, The Christian Science Monitor, The Denver Post, Educational Leadership, Phi Delta Kappan, Education Week*, and many others, as well as three books about mountain climbing and one book about teaching reading. He has been on climbing expeditions to Alaska, Greenland, Tanzania, Peru, Bolivia, Ecuador, Argentina, Mexico, Europe, and Mount Everest. He and his wife Peggy have three daughters and live in Billings, Montana.

While searching for a trail through the thick underbrush near Cheticamp Lake in the Cape Breton Highlands in Nova Scotia, Steve Gardiner found this moose antler. The team eventually located the faint trail and slogged through deep mud from the heavy rains caused by Hurricane Arthur.
Photo by John Jancik.

About John Jancik

John Jancik was born and raised in Wisconsin, but early on was drawn to the mountains and has called Colorado home for more than thirty years. John has climbed on six continents and successfully reached more than sixty-five domestic and international highpoints. In 2002, he co-authored a book (*Under the Midnight Sun*) about his two expeditions to the northernmost land on Earth; North Peary Land, Greenland. A geologist by academic training, he owned an oil and gas exploration service company for over twenty-six years. He and his wife Terri have four children and live in Parker, Colorado.

John Jancik on the summit of Norway's highest peak, Galdhøpiggen. The highest peak in northern Europe, Galdhøpiggen is located in the Jotunheimen region which contains Norway's 29 highest mountains.
Photo by Jessica Morse.

Appendix A
Donations

To make a donation to The Rowell Fund for Tibet, please send a check to the address below or contact The Rowell Fund for Tibet for other options.

THE ROWELL FUND FOR TIBET
c/o The International Campaign For Tibet (ICT)
1825 Jefferson Place NW
Washington, D.C. 20036
Phone: (202) 785-1515
Fax: (202) 785-4343
Website: https://www.savetibet.org/about-ict/rowell-fund-tibet/
E-mail: rowellfund@savetibet.org

Appendix B
Contact Information

INTERNATIONAL CAMPAIGN FOR TIBET (ICT)
1825 Jefferson Place NW
Washington, D.C. 20036
Phone: (202) 785-1515
Fax: (202) 785-4343
Website: http://www.savetibet.org
E-mail: info@savetibet.org

MOUNTAIN LIGHT PHOTOGRAPHY, INC.
Bishop Gallery
106 South Main Street
Bishop, California 93514
Phone: (760) 873-7700
Fax: (760) 873-3980
Website: http://www.mountainlight.com/
E-mail: gallery@mountainlight.com

HIGHPOINTERS CLUB
PO Box 1496, Golden, CO 80402
(303) 278-1915
newsletter@highpointers.org
Website: www.Highpointers.org
Facebook: https://www.facebook.com/Highpointers/

50 FOR TIBET
Website: http://www.50fortibet.org
Facebook: https://www.facebook.com/50fortibet/

Appendix C
Suggested Reading

Gardiner, Steve. (1990). *Why I Climb: Personal Insights from Top Climbers* (contains a chapter about Galen Rowell). Harrisburg: Stackpole Books.

Gilbertson, Matthew. (2013). *The Great Quest: 50 State High Points and More.* AuthorHouse.

Glickman, Joe, and Akerlund, Nels. (2003). *To the Top: Climbing America's 50 State Highpoints.* Northwood Press.

Holmes, Don. (2000). *Highpoints of the United States: A Guide to the Fifty State Highpoints.* Salt Lake City: University of Utah Press.

Jancik, John; Gardiner, Steve; and Richardson, Javana (2002). *Under the Midnight Sun: The Ascent of John Denver Peak and the Search for the Northernmost Land on Earth.* Greenwood Village, CO: StarsEnd Creations.

Rowell, Galen. (1983). *Mountains of the Middle Kingdom.* New York: Random House.

Rowell, Galen. (1996). *The Art of Adventure.* Sierra Club Books.

Rowell, Galen, and His Holiness the 14th Dalai Lama. (1990). *My Tibet.* Berkeley: University of California Press.

Winger, Charles and Winger, Diane. (2002). *Highpoint Adventures: The Complete Guide to the 50 State Highpoints.* Colorado Mountain Club Press.

Appendix D
Letter of Support-Governor Ritter

STATE OF COLORADO

OFFICE OF THE GOVERNOR
136 State Capitol Building
Denver, Colorado 80203
(303) 866 - 2471
(303) 866 - 2003 fax

Bill Ritter, Jr.
Governor

July 23, 2007

On behalf of the citizens of Colorado, I would like to extend my support to Team Highpoint in their pursuit of furthering global awareness.

Team Highpoint is making a difference in the global community. The Team strives to increase awareness by communicating issues of importance to both local and international audiences. As a result of these efforts, many underprivileged persons have been granted opportunities to prosper. Team Highpoint's mission to summit the highest peaks in each of the 50 states is a remarkable task, a task that will inspire others to pursue larger concerns and make a difference in our world.

Again, congratulations on your mission and for supporting global awareness of honorable causes. You have my best wishes now, and in the years to come.

Sincerely,

Bill Ritter, Jr.
Governor

Appendix E
Letter of Support-Mark Udall

MARK UDALL
2ND DISTRICT, COLORADO

100 CANNON HOB
WASHINGTON, D.C. 20515
(202) 225-2161
(202) 226-7840 (FAX)

8601 TURNPIKE DR., #206
WESTMINSTER, CO 80031
(303) 650-7820
(303) 650-7827 (FAX)

291 MAIN ST.
P.O. BOX 325
MINTURN, CO 81645
(970) 827-4154
(970) 827-4138 (FAX)

Congress of the United States
House of Representatives
Washington, DC 20515-0602

COMMITTEE ON ARMED SERVICES
SUBCOMMITTEE ON READINESS
SUBCOMMITTEE ON TERRORISM AND UNCONVENTIONAL THREATS

COMMITTEE ON SCIENCE AND TECHNOLOGY
CHAIRMAN
SUBCOMMITTEE ON SPACE AND AERONAUTICS
SUBCOMMITTEE ON ENERGY AND ENVIRONMENT

COMMITTEE ON NATURAL RESOURCES
SUBCOMMITTEE ON WATER AND POWER
SUBCOMMITTEE ON NATIONAL PARKS, FORESTS, AND PUBLIC LANDS

October 16, 2007

http://markudall.house.gov/HoR/CoO2/home

Dear Friends,

On behalf of Colorado's 2nd Congressional District, I'm pleased to write this letter of support for 50 For Tibet and the Colorado-based Team Highpoint. As a fundraising effort for The Rowell Fund for Tibet, the goal of Team Highpoint is to reach the highest points in all 50 states. Since June of 2006, the Team has climbed over 76,000 feet of elevation, traveled over 60,000 miles, and reached 47 state highpoints, including Washington, D.C.

The purpose of this effort is to help communicate important Tibetan community issues to the broader Tibetan population and to a national audience, as well as to preserve Tibetan culture in the face of the Chinese occupation. Every year, grants are awarded to Tibetans pursuing interests such as photography, film-making, writing, journalism, and projects that promote these skills within the Tibetan community.

As someone who has had the opportunity to travel extensively throughout Asia, I feel a deep connection with that part of the world. I have spent time in Tibet, getting to know the people and sharing in their customs and traditions. The Tibetans are a peaceful and spiritual people, and the preservation of Tibet's unique cultural heritage enriches our global community. Team Highpoint/50 for Tibet is making a positive and essential difference in the lives of Tibetans, and their efforts deserve special praise.

I support Team Highpoint's work wholeheartedly and hope that others will give this organization every consideration.

Warm Regards,

Mark Udall
Member of Congress

Appendix F
Letter of Support-ICT

INTERNATIONAL CAMPAIGN FOR TIBET

INTERNATIONAL COUNCIL OF ADVISORS
HARRISON FORD
VACLAV HAVEL
HIDEAKI KASE
KERRY KENNEDY
VYTAUTAS LANDSBERGIS
FANG LIZHI
MAIREAD MAGUIRE
ADOLFO PEREZ ESQUIVEL
JOSE RAMOS-HORTA
RABI RAY
PROFESSOR SAMDHONG RINPOCHE
SULAK SIVARAKSA
TENZIN N. TETHONG
DESMOND TUTU
ELIE WIESEL

BOARD OF DIRECTORS
RICHARD GERE, CHAIRMAN
LODI G. GYARI, EXECUTIVE CHAIRMAN

WASHINGTON OFFICE
MARY BETH MARKEY, PRESIDENT
BHUCHUNG K. TSERING, VICE PRESIDENT FOR SPECIAL PROGRAMS

1825 JEFFERSON PLACE, NW
WASHINGTON, DC 20036
202.785.1515
202.785.4343 FAX
INFO@SAVETIBET.ORG
WWW.SAVETIBET.ORG

INTERNATIONAL OFFICES
AMSTERDAM
BERLIN
BRUSSELS

FIELD OFFICES
DHARAMSALA
KATHMANDU

April 15, 2011

Dear Friend of Tibet,

I'm writing to express my wholehearted support for Team Highpoint and the "50 for Tibet" project. Since "50 for Tibet" began as a distinct volunteer-led effort in 2006, the team has raised approximately $200,000 in donations for the International Campaign for Tibet's Rowell Fund. The Rowell Fund is an important part of our work because it allows ICT to nurture initiative and creativity in Tibetan communities with small grants that invoke the legacy of Barbara and Galen Rowell's passion for Tibet. Since its inception in 2003, the Rowell Fund has awarded over $285,000 in grants to over 80 Tibetan grantees.

Since June of 2006, Team Highpoint has completed 48 of 50 highpoint climbs in the United States and has even completed a few extra expeditions over the years including the highpoints in Scotland, Wales, Northern Ireland, England and Ireland. Later this year, they plan to climb Gannett Peak in Wyoming and peaks in Norway, Sweden, Finland and Denmark. Along the way, Team Highpoint has done an excellent job raising awareness of the Tibet issue with the media and individuals they've encountered while climbing. Their commitment to this issue and their dedication to the memory of Barbara and Galen Rowell is inspiring.

To learn more about the "50 for Tibet" project and Team Highpoint, please visit www.50forTibet.org. You can also learn more about the International Campaign for Tibet at www.savetibet.org.

With your support Team Highpoint can continue to summit for Tibet! Please consider making a contribution to this marvelous project.

Sincerely,

Mary Beth Markey
President
International Campaign for Tibet

Appendix G
Letter of Support-Jimmy Chin

November 26, 2012

Jimmy Chin

PO Box 1045

Victor ID 83455

To Whom It May Concern:

As a board member of the Rowell Fund for Tibet, I wanted to pledge my support of John Jancik and his tremendous efforts through his climbing project, 50 for Tibet, to fundraise for the Rowell Fund for Tibet. John and 50 for Tibet have been critically important to the Rowell Fund for Tibet over the years and I hope he has continued success with his climbing aspirations and fundraising.

Sincerely,

Jimmy Chin